FREE? FONTS
FREEWARE & SHAREWARE
FONT DIRECTORY

Edited by
Steve Campbell & Marie Campbell

Free?Fonts
Freeware & Shareware Font Directory

ISBN-13: 978-0-9552431-0-3

Published, designed and typeset
by Début Publications Ltd 2006

Cover design by tallkids.co.uk

Printed in the UK by Unwin Brothers, Surrey.

Contents

Introduction

What follows is a reference to, and a very small selection of the hundreds of freeware and shareware fonts available for free download, with links to the Font Foundries and Type Designers who created them.

The fonts are showcased in an easy to read index alongside Designer's credits, font category and details of the licence agreement in the form of a Read Me file, punctuated by sample artwork of a selection of the fonts in context.

Many, although not all, of the fonts showcased in this book are provided by Designers and Foundries who also produce commercial typefaces. We urge you to visit the web address provided with each listing to browse the many diverse approaches to contemporary Type Design and to show your support and appreciation.

Début Publications Ltd
January 2006

Metal fonts of a half century ago took years to develop and sold for thousands of dollars. Phototype fonts of a few decades ago still took nearly as long to develop but the price dropped to hundreds of dollars. Today, digital fonts typically take less than a year – sometimes only a few weeks or days – to develop and most are priced well below $50, or in some cases, given away free or as try-before-you-buy shareware.

Digital font technology has made it possible. Anyone with the slightest interest can buy a copy of FontLab or Fontographer and become a type founder. This does not mean it is easy to create a font. Nor is it easy to make a living making fonts. Nobody's getting rich off it. For most people who do it, it does not pay enough for them to quit their day job. I am one of the lucky few who has managed to get to a point where I do make my living at it, and it took fifteen years to get there.

Good quality commercial fonts take considerable time and effort to build, test and debug. These are not the kind that only take a few days to make. When you pay money for a font, you rightly expect that it will have a complete character set and kerning, and will perform flawlessly. So, if it can be so much work to make a font, why would someone give it away? In some cases, it is because the author knows the fonts are not up to commercial font standards and wouldn't feel right charging money. But this is not the only possibility.

For me it depends on the history and intended use of the font. While I am primarily in the business of making commercial fonts, I do offer a few commercial-quality free fonts, including one called Anonymous™. This is a monospaced font originally intended as a replacement for Monaco, a Macintosh system font. Anonymous™ started out as a freeware 'bitmap' font designed by a friend of mine. As a bitmap font, it worked well on-screen, but was pretty useless for print-outs. She wondered if I would make a scaleable 'outline' version that could be used for printing. Eventually, I did. The result is my Anonymous™ TrueType font. As the author of this font, I could have chosen to go commercial and sell it, but since the original was a freeware font, and since it is a replacement for a 'free' system font, it made sense to me to keep the TrueType version free.

Still, I don't think of it just as a free font. I also think of it as a free sample of my work. It draws traffic to my site and some of these visitors may be interested in purchasing one of my commercial fonts. The font has become popular with programmers. As a group, programmers probably do not buy many fonts, but it is gratifying to know they have found it useful.

Every shareware or freeware font developer has such a story. Some are enthusiasts or dabblers who do it as a hobby. Some are novices who hope one day to 'go commercial' and want to share their early attempts. Some are professional font developers who do it to promote themselves. Some are scholars who create special fonts for their area of study and want to share them with their colleagues. Some are idealists who have the time and resources to build fonts and make them available to those who need them.

Whatever the reason, shareware and freeware fonts are released that way because that's what their authors chose to do. Fonts, whether commercial or not, are software, and as software are protected by copyright. What this

means is that the author has the right to say how a font may be distributed. This is normally spelled out in the font licence included with a font (in the case of shareware and freeware fonts, it may be found in a 'Read Me' file). The existence of freeware and shareware fonts does not mean that commercial fonts are a rip-off. It is all about author's intent.

When you consider the fonts shown in this book, also consider the person behind the font. Go to their website, find out what they are about. After all, they are sharing their work with you.

Mark Simonson
ms-studio.com
December 2005

Licensing Agreements

All the fonts listed in this publication are either freeware or shareware and must be used in accordance with the licence agreements set out by the Foundry/Type Designer. For your convenience, each of the listings includes information on this licence under the heading 'Read Me'.

There are a few basic rules that any user of font software must be aware of before using fonts. These rules can vary between licence agreements and are only shown here as a guide. If you are in any doubt as to the limitations placed on the font software, please contact the Designer directly.

1. Anyone using font software must have a licence (see 4&5).

2. Font software is not purchased, it is licenced. Your font licence grants you limited use from the Type Designer or Publisher.

3. This licence is granted in the form of an 'End User Licence Agreement' and usually accompanies the font in the form of a 'Read Me' file.

4. The majority of agreements do not allow you to make copies of, or distribute font software to anyone who does not have their own licence (this includes design agencies and printers).

5. You will be liable if you re-distribute font software to others to use without a licence.

Hearst

Heimchen (Das Gute)

Horse Puke

Hurry Up

Interplanetary Crap

Jack's Mannequin

Kenyan Coffee

Komodore

Libel Suit

Max Rhodes

Memory Lapses

Misproject

Motherfunker

Mulder handwriting

Nail Scratch

Nasty

Neasden PIP

P22 Sinel

P22 Typewriter

Pagra

Pastelaria

Paulchen

Perlon

Porcelain

Pricedown

Prime Minister of Canada

Pupcat

Queen of Pain

Record

Respress Capitals

Rochester

Selfish

Sexsmith

Shamools

Shortcut

Space Age

Splurge

Stentiga

Street Cred

Subamera

Subelair

Subeve

Suboel

Sybil Green

The Time of the
Revolving Door and Friends

Thicket

TicketCapitals

UniF

Velvenda Cooler

You're Gone

Zrnic

Abuse

ABCDEFGHIJKLMNOPQRSTUVWXYZ
ABCDEFGHIJKLMNOPQRSTUVWXYZ
0123456789 (.,;:?!$&−*) {@"#%'+/\[<>=]^_`|~€}

Weights Available: REGULAR

Designer: Damien Gosset

Website: www.daaams.fr.st

Platform PC, Mac

Category: Script, Graffiti

Date of Creation: Information not provided

Additional Information: Other commercial, freeware & shareware fonts are available from the same source. Please visit the designer's website for more information.

Read Me: This is a 'Drinkware' font, it can be used for free for your personal use only, and if you're nice you can send me a bottle of local beer (and don't hesitate to send me samples of your work, made with this font).

A Read Me file accompanies this font, always keep these files together.

If you want to use Abuse for commercial purposes, please drop me an e-mail.

Direct URL: www.dafont.com/font.php?file=abuse

Anonymous™

abcdefghijklmnopqrstuvwxyz
ABCDEFGHIJKLMNOPQRSTUVWXYZ
Ø123456789 (.,;:?!$&-*)
{@"#%'+/\[<>=]^_`|~€}

Weights Available: Regular

Designer: Mark Simonson

Website: www.ms-studio.com

Platform: PC, Mac

Category: Monospace Sans Serif

Date of Creation: 2001

Additional Information: This font is intended as an alternative to Apple's Monaco system font. Other commercial fonts are available from the designer's website.

Read Me: Anonymous™ can be freely distributed as long as it is not modified and the Read Me file accompanies the font file.

Anonymous™ may not be sold or offered for sale, or included with another software product offered for sale, except with our express written permission. Online services and bulletin boards may make it available to their users at no charge other than the normal connection fees.

Non-profit user groups which hold regularly scheduled public meetings may distribute it at no charge.

Print, CD-ROM, and text magazines may publish it on CD-ROM, floppy disk, binhexed or zipped where applicable, without our prior consent, as long as we each receive a copy of the issue containing our font within two months of release of the magazine. CD-ROM or floppy disk shareware/freeware/public domain collections may include it without our prior consent, as long as we each receive a copy of the CD-ROM or floppy collection within two months of release of the collection.

Direct URL: www.ms-studio.com/FontSales/anonymous.html

ABCDEFGHIJKLMNOPQRSTUUWXYZ
ABCDEFGHIJKLMNOPQRSTUUWXYZ
0123456789 [.,;:?!-×] '''"+/\[=]_

Weights Available: REGULAR

Designer: Boris Moser

Website: www.helldunkel.com

Platform: PC

Category: Display

Date of Creation: 2005

Additional Information: Other freeware & shareware fonts are available from the same source. Please visit the designer's website for more information.

Read Me: All helldunkel.com fonts are freeware. You can do whatever the heck you want to do with them – which includes for private or commercial use, just enjoy.

Direct URL: www.helldunkel.com/2005/set.htm

Astonished

abcdefghijklmnopqrstuvwxyz
ABCDEFGHIJKLMNOPQRSTUVWXYZ
0123456789 (..:;?!$&-*) {@"#%'+/\[<>=]^_`|~Đ}

Weights Available: Regular

Designer: Eduardo Recife

Website: www.misprintedtype.com

Platform: PC, Mac

Category: Grunge, Display

Date of Creation: 1998-2004

Additional Information: Other freeware & shareware fonts are available from the same source. Please visit the designer's website.

Read Me: This is a freeware typeface and can be used on your commercial or non-commercial work for free. But here is a list of things you could do, only if you want to:

Link www.misprintedtype.com on your site, send me a sample of the work you did using my typeface, mail me some printed material using my typeface, credit 'misprinted type' on your work, donate money, books, cds, artwork, whatever you want.

DO NOT: Sell this font or modify it.

DO NOT: Redistribute this font without my permission.

Direct URL: www.misprintedtype.com/v3/fonts.php

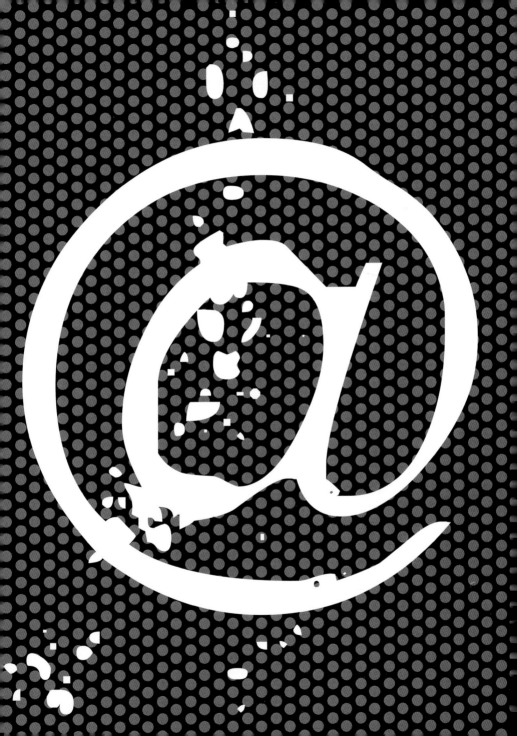

Baveuse

aBCDeFGHIJKLMNOPQRSTUVWXYZ
aBCDeFGHIJKLMNOPQRSTUVWXYZ
0123456789 [.,;:?!$&-*] @"#%'+/\[<>=]_ `|€

Font Family: Baveuse Regular, Baveuse 3D Regular

....

Designer: Ray Larabie

Website: www.larabiefonts.com

Platform: PC, Mac

Category: Decorative, Display

Date of Creation: 2000

Additional Information: Other freeware & shareware fonts are available from the same source and commercial fonts are available from the same designer at www.typodermic.com.

....

Read Me: This font is free to use for personal and/or commercial purposes. No payment is necessary but a sample of your product would be gratefully appreciated so I can see how the font looks in use.

If you'd like to make a voluntary donation to Larabie Fonts for the use of the free fonts in any amount please go to www.larabiefonts.com/donation.html.

Some Larabie fonts have enhanced and expanded families available for sale at: www.typodermic.com.

NB: A complete licence agreement is enclosed with each 'Larabie' font downloaded.

....

Direct URL: www.myfonts.com/fonts/larabie/baveuse/

abcdeffghijklmnopaRstuvwxyz
abcdeffghijklmnopaRstuvwxyz
0123456789 (.,;:?!$&-*) (∂"‡'+/\[()=]_)

Weights Available: **regular**

Designer: Lopetz

Website: www.burodestruct.net

Platform: PC, Mac

Category: Headline

Date of Creation: 2001

Additional Information: Other freeware, shareware and commercial fonts are available from the same source. Please visit the designer's website for more information.

Read Me: Büro Destruct free fonts are free to use in all your designs, commercial or non commercial. While they are free, they are not in the public domain and remain in the exclusive property of Büro Destruct. The free and non free Büro Destruct fonts may not be redistributed in any way (they may not be resold, distributed commercially, they may not be made available for download) without the written permission of Büro Destruct.

Büro Destruct shall, in no event, be liable for any damages arising out of the usage of Büro Destruct fonts.

NB: A complete licence agreement is enclosed with each 'Büro Destruct' font downloaded.

Direct URL: www.typedifferent.com/2001/

BD Kalinka

abcdefghijklmnopqrstuvwxyz

ABCDEFGHijKLMNOPO.RSTUVWXYZ

0123456789 (.,;:?!$8-*) (@"#%+/\<>=Γ_TE)

Weights Available: Regular

Designer: Heiwid

Website: www.burodestruct.net

Platform: PC, Mac

Category: Headline

Date of Creation: 2005

Additional Information: Other freeware, shareware and commercial fonts are available from the same source. Please visit the designer's website for more information.

Read Me: Büro Destruct free fonts are free to use in all your designs, commercial or non commercial. While they are free, they are not in the public domain and remain in the exclusive property of Büro Destruct. The free and non free Büro Destruct fonts may not be redistributed in any way (they may not be resold, distributed commercially, they may not be made available for download) without the written permission of Büro Destruct.

Büro Destruct shall, in no event, be liable for any damages arising out of the usage of Büro Destruct fonts.

NB: A complete licence agreement is enclosed with each 'Büro Destruct' font downloaded.

Direct URL: www.typedifferent.com/2005/

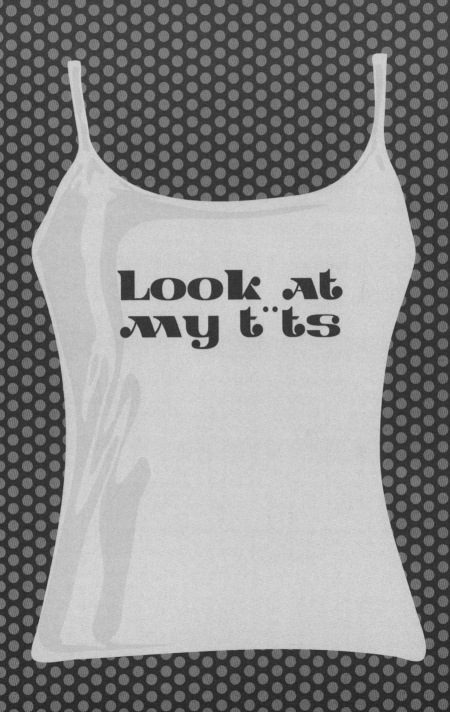

Berylium

abcdefghijklmnopqrstuvwxyz
ABCDEFGHIJKLMNOPQRSTUVWXYZ
0123456789 (.,;:?!$&-*) {@"#%'+/\[<>=]^_`|€}

Weights Available: Regular, *Italic,* **Bold,** ***Bold Italic***

Designer: Ray Larabie

Website: www.larabiefonts.com

Platform: PC, Mac

Category: Garalde

Date of Creation: 2000

Additional Information: Other freeware & shareware fonts are available from the same source and commercial fonts are available from the same designer at www.typodermic.com.

Read Me: This font is free to use for personal and/or commercial purposes. No payment is necessary but a sample of your product would be gratefully appreciated so I can see how the font looks in use.

If you'd like to make a voluntary donation to Larabie Fonts for the use of the free fonts in any amount please go to www.larabiefonts.com/donation.html.

Some Larabie fonts have enhanced and expanded families available for sale at: www.typodermic.com.

NB: A complete licence agreement is enclosed with each 'Larabie' font downloaded.

Direct URL: www.myfonts.com/fonts/larabie/berylium/

abcdefghijklmnopqrstuvwxyz
ABCDEFGHIJKLMNOPQRSTUVWXYZ
0123456789 [.,:;?!$&-*] @"#%'+/\<>=^_'~

Weights Available: Regular

Designer: Ray Larabie

Website: www.larabiefonts.com

Platform: PC, Mac

Category: Funny

Date of Creation: 1997

Additional Information: Other freeware & shareware fonts are available from the same source and commercial fonts are available from the same designer at www.typodermic.com.

Read Me: This font is free to use for personal and/or commercial purposes. No payment is necessary but a sample of your product would be gratefully appreciated so I can see how the font looks in use.

If you'd like to make a voluntary donation to Larabie Fonts for the use of the free fonts in any amount please go to www.larabiefonts.com/donation.html.

Some Larabie fonts have enhanced and expanded families available for sale at: www.typodermic.com.

NB: A complete licence agreement is enclosed with each 'Larabie' font downloaded.

Direct URL: www.myfonts.com/fonts/larabie/biometric-joe/

Birdland Aeroplane

abcdefghijklmnopqrstuvwxyz
ABCDEFGHIJKLMNOPQRSTUVWXYZ
0123456789 [.,;:?!$&-*] [("#%'+/\<>=]_`^€]

Weights Available: **Regular, bold**

....

Designer: Ray Larabie

Website: www.larabiefonts.com

Platform: PC, Mac

Category: Funny

Date of Creation: 1998

Additional Information: Other freeware &
shareware fonts are available from the same
source and commercial fonts are available from
the same designer at www.typodermic.com.

....

Read Me: This font is free to use for personal and/or commercial purposes. No payment
is necessary but a sample of your product would be gratefully appreciated so I can see how
the font looks in use.

If you'd like to make a voluntary donation to Larabie Fonts for the use of the free fonts
in any amount please go to www.larabiefonts.com/donation.html.

Some Larabie fonts have enhanced and expanded families available for sale
at: www.typodermic.com.

NB: A complete licence agreement is enclosed with each 'Larabie' font downloaded.

....

Direct URL: www.myfonts.com/fonts/larabie/birdland-aeroplane/

ABCDEFGHIJKLMNOPQRSTUVWXYZ
ABCDEFGHIJKLMNOPQRSTUVWXYZ
0123456789 [.,:?!$6 −*] ←@”#%'+∧[<>=]_`£→

Font Family: BRAESIDE LUMBERBOY REGULAR, BRAESIDE OUTLINE REGULAR

Designer: Ray Larabie

Website: www.larabiefonts.com

Platform: PC, Mac

Category: Decorative

Date of Creation: 1998

Additional Information: Other freeware & shareware fonts are available from the same source and commercial fonts are available from the same designer at www.typodermic.com.

Read Me: This font is free to use for personal and/or commercial purposes. No payment is necessary but a sample of your product would be gratefully appreciated so I can see how the font looks in use.

If you'd like to make a voluntary donation to Larabie Fonts for the use of the free fonts in any amount please go to www.larabiefonts.com/donation.html.

Some Larabie fonts have enhanced and expanded families available for sale at: www.typodermic.com.

NB: A complete licence agreement is enclosed with each 'Larabie' font downloaded.

Direct URL: www.myfonts.com/fonts/larabie/braeside/

Broken 15

abcdefghijklmnopqrstuvwxyz
ABCDEFGHIJKLMNOPQRSTUVWXYZ
0123456789 (.,:?!$&-*) {@"#%+/\[<>=]^_|~D}

Weights Available: Regular

Designer: Eduardo Recife

Website: www.misprintedtype.com

Platform: PC, Mac

Category: Grunge, Display

Date of Creation: 1998-2004

Additional Information: Other freeware & shareware fonts are available from the same source. Please visit the designer's website.

Read Me: This is a freeware typeface and can be used on your commercial or non-commercial work for free. But here is a list of things you could do, only if you want to:

Link www.misprintedtype.com on your site, send me a sample of the work you did using my typeface, mail me some printed material using my typeface, credit 'misprinted type' on your work, donate money, books, cds, artwork, whatever you want.

DO NOT: Sell this font or modify it.

DO NOT: Redistribute this font without my permission.

Direct URL: www.misprintedtype.com/v3/fonts.php

CA Koenigsbrueck

abcdefghijklmnopqrstuvwxyz
ABCDEFGHIJKLMNOPQRSTUVWXYZ
0123456789 .,:!@

Weights Available: *Regular*

Designer: Stefan Claudius

Website: www.cape-arcona.com

Platform: PC, Mac

Category: Handwriting, Script

Date of Creation: Information not provided

Additional Information: Other freeware, shareware and commercial fonts are available from the same source. Please visit the designer's website for more information.

Read Me: No payment is required for this Cape-Arcona Type Foundry font. This font is free for all non-commercial uses. If you use it in a commercial way, a donation would be appreciated.

This font may not be sold or re-distributed.

You may not modify, adapt, translate, reverse engineer, decompile, disassemble, alter or otherwise copy this font.

Except for your right to use this font, all other rights are owned and retained by Cape-Arcona Type Foundry.

Cape-Arcona Type Foundry is not liable for any damage resulting from the use of this font.

NB: A complete licence agreement is enclosed with each 'Cape-Arcona' font downloaded.

Direct URL: www.cape-arcona.com

CA Traktor

ABCDEFGHIJKLMNOPQRSTUVWXYZ
ABCDEFGHIJKLMNOPQRSTUVWXYZ
0123456789 (.,;:?!$&-*) {'"'U/\[‹›]_|}

Weights Available: **REGULAR**

Designer: Stefan Claudius

Website: www.cape-arcona.com

Platform: PC, Mac

Category: Grotesque, Display

Date of Creation: Information not provided

Additional Information: Other freeware & shareware and commercial fonts are available from the same source. Please visit the designer's website for more information.

Read Me: No payment is required for this Cape-Arcona Type Foundry font. This font is free for all non-commercial uses. If you use it in a commercial way, a donation would be appreciated.

This font may not be sold or re-distributed.

You may not modify, adapt, translate, reverse engineer, decompile, disassemble, alter or otherwise copy this font.

Except for your right to use this font, all other rights are owned and retained by Cape-Arcona Type Foundry.

Cape-Arcona Type Foundry is not liable for any damage resulting from the use of this font.

NB: A complete licence agreement is enclosed with each 'Cape-Arcona' font downloaded.

Direct URL: www.cape-arcona.com

LINE DO NOT CROSS POLICE

POLICE LINE DO NOT CROSS PO

Cafe 405

ABCDEFGHIJKLMNOPQRSTUVWXYZ
ABCDEFGHIJKLMNOPQRSTUVWXYZ
0123456789 (.,:?!$&-*) {@"#%'+/\[<>=]^_`|~}

Weights Available: VANDAL STYLE

Designer: Kent Hertzog

Website: www.digitallybranded.com

Platform: PC, Mac

Category: Pixel

Date of Creation: 2003

Additional Information: Other freeware & shareware fonts are available from the same source. Please visit the designer's website.

NB: There is no Read Me file accompanying this font, however, all Digitally Branded fonts are fully freeware. Do not sell or modify the font and please respect the designer's rights. If there are any queries as to how this font can be used please contact the designer directly.

Direct URL: www.digitallybranded.com/v3/v3.html

Camouflarsch

ABCDEFGHIJKLMNOPQRST UVWXYZ
ABCDEFGHIJKLMNOPQRST UVWXYZ
0123456789 [.,;?!-*] +/=

Weights Available: REGULAR, **BOLD**

Designer: Boris Moser

Website: www.helldunkel.com

Platform: PC

Category: Grunge, Display

Date of Creation: 2005

Additional Information: Other freeware & shareware fonts are available from the same source. Please visit the designer's website.

Read Me: All helldunkel.com fonts are freeware. You can do whatever the heck you want to do with them – which includes for private or commercial use, just enjoy.

Direct URL: www.helldunkel.com/2005/set.htm

Casi

abcdefghijklmnopqrstuvwxyz
abcdefghijklmnopqrstuvwxyz
0123456789 (.,;:?!\$&-*) {@"#%'+/\[<>=]^_`|~∂}

Weights Available: *Regular*

Designer: Nina David

Website: www.font-o-rama.com

Platform: PC, Mac

Category: Serif

Date of Creation: 2000

Additional Information: Other freeware, shareware and commercial fonts are available from the same source.

Please visit the designer's website.

Read Me: This typeface is for free and meant 'as is'. You can copy and give it away to your friends as long as this Read Me file is included with the postscript data.

Don't try to distribute it!

Direct URL: www.font-o-rama.com/free_fonts/casi.html

abcdefghijklmnopqrstuvwxyz
ABCDEFGHIJKLMNOPQRSTUVWXYZ
0123456789 (.,:;'!$¢-#) @"#%+/◇= `

Weights Available: *Regular*

Designer: Ray Larabie	**Date of Creation:** 2000
Website: www.larabiefonts.com	**Additional Information:** Other freeware & shareware fonts are available from the same source and commercial fonts are available from the same designer at www.typodermic.com.
Platform: PC, Mac	
Category: Script	

Read Me: This font is free to use for personal and/or commercial purposes. No payment is necessary but a sample of your product would be gratefully appreciated so I can see how the font looks in use.

If you'd like to make a voluntary donation to Larabie Fonts for the use of the free fonts in any amount please go to www.larabiefonts.com/donation.html.

Some Larabie fonts have enhanced and expanded families available for sale at: www.typodermic.com.

NB: A complete licence agreement is enclosed with each 'Larabie' font downloaded.

Direct URL: www.myfonts.com/fonts/larabie/cretino/

Cricket

abcdefghijklmnopqrstuvwxyz
ABCDEFGHIJKLM NoPQRSTUVWXYZ
0123456789 (.,?!\$¢—*) {@"#%'+/\[<>=]^_~}

Weights Available: Regular

Designer: Amy E. Conger

Website: www.abecedarienne.com

Platform: PC, Mac

Category: Hand lettered

Date of Creation: 1997

Additional Information: Other freeware & shareware fonts are available from the same source. Please visit the designer's website.

Read Me: You may distribute this font shamelessly. You may translate it to any platform, just don't change the name. You may remix it, just give me credit and let me know.

Direct URL: www.abecedarienne.com/index.shtml#cricket

An ode to the Ill-fated Ms. Raglan
& her Unfortunate Friend

A chimney pot fell off the roof
And landed on her head.
I wonder who will feed the cat
Now poor Ms. Raglan's dead.

Crystal Radio Kit

abcdefghijklmnopqrstuvwxyz
ABCDEFGHIJKLMNOPQRSTUVWXYZ
0123456789 (.,:;?!$&-*) @"`#%'+/\ <>=^_~

Weights Available: Regular

Designer: Ray Larabie

Website: www.larabiefonts.com

Platform: PC, Mac

Category: Funny

Date of Creation: 1998

Additional Information: Other freeware & shareware fonts are available from the same source and commercial fonts are available from the same designer at www.typodermic.com.

Read Me: This font is free to use for personal and/or commercial purposes. No payment is necessary but a sample of your product would be gratefully appreciated so I can see how the font looks in use.

If you'd like to make a voluntary donation to Larabie Fonts for the use of the free fonts in any amount please go to www.larabiefonts.com/donation.html.

Some Larabie fonts have enhanced and expanded families available for sale at: www.typodermic.com.

NB: A complete licence agreement is enclosed with each 'Larabie' font downloaded.

Direct URL: www.myfonts.com/fonts/larabie/crystal-radio-kit/

Cuomotype

abcdefghijklmnopqrstuvwxyz
ABCDEFGHIJKLMNOPQRSTUVWXYZ
0123456789 (.,;:?!$&-*) {@"#%'+/\[< > =]_`|~}

Weights Available: Regular

Designer: Ray Larabie

Website: www.larabiefonts.com

Platform: PC, Mac

Category: Funny

Date of Creation: 1998

Additional Information: Other freeware & shareware fonts are available from the same source and commercial fonts are available from the same designer at www.typodermic.com.

Read Me: This font is free to use for personal and/or commercial purposes. No payment is necessary but a sample of your product would be gratefully appreciated so I can see how the font looks in use.

If you'd like to make a voluntary donation to Larabie Fonts for the use of the free fonts in any amount please go to www.larabiefonts.com/donation.html.

Some Larabie fonts have enhanced and expanded families available for sale at: www.typodermic.com.

NB: A complete licence agreement is enclosed with each 'Larabie' font downloaded.

Direct URL: www.myfonts.com/fonts/larabie/cuomotype/

abcdefghijklmnopqrstuvwxyz
ABCDEFGHIJKLMNOPQRSTUVWXYZ
0123456789 (.,;:?!$&-×) {@"#%'+/\[<>=]^_|~£}

Weights Available: **Normal**

Designer: Boris Moser

Website: www.helldunkel.com

Platform: PC

Category: Display

Date of Creation: 2005

Additional Information: Other freeware & shareware fonts are available from the same source. Please visit the designer's website.

Read Me: All helldunkel.com fonts are freeware. You can do whatever the heck you want to do with them – which includes for private or commercial use, just enjoy.

Direct URL: www.helldunkel.com/2005/set.htm

Delta Hey Max Nine

abcdefghijklmnopqrstuvwxyz

ABCDEFGHIJKLMNOPQRSTUVWXYZ

0123456789 (.,::?!$&-*) @"#%'*/\‹›¬`_

Weights Available: Regular

Designer: Ray Larabie

Website: www.larabiefonts.com

Platform: PC, Mac

Category: Funny

Date of Creation: 1998

Additional Information: Other freeware & shareware fonts are available from the same source and commercial fonts are available from the same designer at www.typodermic.com.

Read Me: This font is free to use for personal and/or commercial purposes. No payment is necessary but a sample of your product would be gratefully appreciated so I can see how the font looks in use.

If you'd like to make a voluntary donation to Larabie Fonts for the use of the free fonts in any amount please go to www.larabiefonts.com/donation.html.

Some Larabie fonts have enhanced and expanded families available for sale at: www.typodermic.com.

NB: A complete licence agreement is enclosed with each 'Larabie' font downloaded.

Direct URL: www.myfonts.com/fonts/larabie/delta-hey-max-nine/

Diesel

abcdefghijklmnopqrstuvwxyz
ABCDEFGHIJKLMNOPQRSTUVWXYZ
0123456789 (.,:?!$&-*) {@"#%'+/\[<>=]^_`|~Đ}

Weights Available: Regular

Designer: Eduardo Recife

Website: www.misprintedtype.com

Platform: PC, Mac

Category: Grunge, Display

Date of Creation: 1998-2003

Additional Information: Other freeware & shareware fonts are available from the same source. Please visit the designer's website.

Read Me: This is a freeware typeface and can be used on your commercial or non-commercial work for free. But here is a list of things you could do, only if you want to:

Link www.misprintedtype.com on your site, send me a sample of the work you did using my typeface, mail me some printed material using my typeface, credit 'misprinted type' on your work, donate money, books, cds, artwork, whatever you want.

DO NOT: Sell this font or modify it.

DO NOT: Redistribute this font without my permission.

Direct URL: www.misprintedtype.com/v3/fonts.php

Dirty Ego

ABCDEFGHIJKLMNOPQRSTUVWXYZ
ABCDEFGHIJKLMNOPQRSTUVWXYZ
0123456789 (.,;:?!$&-') [@"#%'+/\[<>=]^`|~€}

Weights Available: REGULAR

Designer: Eduardo Recife

Website: www.misprintedtype.com

Platform: PC, Mac

Category: Grunge, Display

Date of Creation: 1998-2003

Additional Information: Other freeware & shareware fonts are available from the same source. Please visit the designer's website.

Read Me: This is a freeware typeface and can be used on your commercial or non-commercial work for free. But here is a list of things you could do, only if you want to:

Link www.misprintedtype.com on your site, send me a sample of the work you did using my typeface, mail me some printed material using my typeface, credit 'misprinted type' on your work, donate money, books, cds, artwork, whatever you want.

DO NOT: Sell this font or modify it.

DO NOT: Redistribute this font without my permission.

Direct URL: www.misprintedtype.com/v3/fonts.php

abcdefghijklmnopqrstuvwxyz
ABCDEFGHIJKLMNOPQRSTUVWXYZ
①②③④⑤⑥⑦⑧⑨ (.,;:?!$-○) @"%'+/\[=]^_`|~£

Weights Available: Regular

Designer: Eduardo Recife

Website: www.misprintedtype.com.com

Platform: PC, Mac

Category: Grunge, Display

Date of Creation: 1998-2003

Additional Information: Other freeware & shareware fonts are available from the same source. Please visit the designer's website.

Read Me: This is a freeware typeface and can be used on your commercial or non-commercial work for free. But here is a list of things you could do, only if you want to:

Link www.misprintedtype.com on your site, send me a sample of the work you did using my typeface, mail me some printed material using my typeface, credit 'misprinted type' on your work, donate money, books, cds, artwork, whatever you want.

DO NOT: Sell this font or modify it.

DO NOT: Redistribute this font without my permission.

Direct URL: www.misprintedtype.com/v3/fonts.php

Downcome

ABCDEFGHIJKLMNOPQRSTUVWXYZ
ABCDEFGHIJKLMNOPQRSTUVWXYZ
0123456789 (.,;:?!$& -*) {@"#%'+/\[<>=]^_`|~﷯}

Weights Available: REGULAR

Designer: Eduardo Recife

Website: www.misprintedtype.com

Platform: PC, Mac

Category: Grunge, Display

Date of Creation: 1998-2003

Additional Information: Other freeware & shareware fonts are available from the same source. Please visit the designer's website.

Read Me: This is a freeware typeface and can be used on your commercial or non-commercial work for free. But here is a list of things you could do, only if you want to:

Link www.misprintedtype.com on your site, send me a sample of the work you did using my typeface, mail me some printed material using my typeface, credit 'misprinted type' on your work, donate money, books, cds, artwork, whatever you want.

DO NOT: Sell this font or modify it.

DO NOT: Redistribute this font without my permission.

Direct URL: www.misprintedtype.com/v3/fonts.php

abcdefghijklmnopqrstuvwxyz
ABCDEFGHIJKLMNOPQRSTUVWXYZ
0123456789 [.,:;?!$&-*] {@"#%'+/\[<>=]^ `|€}

Weights Available: Regular, *Italic,* **Bold,** ***Bold Italic***

Designer: Ray Larabie	**Date of Creation:** 2000
Website: www.larabiefonts.com	**Additional Information:** Other freeware & shareware fonts are available from the same source and commercial fonts are available from the same designer at www.typodermic.com.
Platform: PC, Mac	
Category: Decorative, Sans Serif	

Read Me: This font is free to use for personal and/or commercial purposes. No payment is necessary but a sample of your product would be gratefully appreciated so I can see how the font looks in use.

If you'd like to make a voluntary donation to Larabie Fonts for the use of the free fonts in any amount please go to www.larabiefonts.com/donation.html.

Some Larabie fonts have enhanced and expanded families available for sale at: www.typodermic.com.

NB: A complete licence agreement is enclosed with each 'Larabie' font downloaded.

Direct URL: www.myfonts.com/fonts/larabie/dream-orphans/

DSC

ABCDEFGHIJKLMNOPQRSTUVWXYZ
ABCDEFGHIJKLMNOPQRSTUVWXYZ
0123456789 (.,;:?!$&-*) {@"#%'+/\[<>=]^_`|~}

Weights Available: REGULAR

Designer: Nina David	**Date of Creation:** 2000
Website: www.font-o-rama.com	**Additional Information:** Other freeware,
Platform: PC, Mac	shareware and commercial fonts are available from the same source.
Category: Pixel	Please visit the designer's website.

Read Me: This typeface is for free and meant 'as is'. You can copy and give it away to your friends as long as this Read Me file is included with the postscript data.

Don't try to distribute it!

Direct URL: www.font-o-rama.com/free_fonts/dsc.html

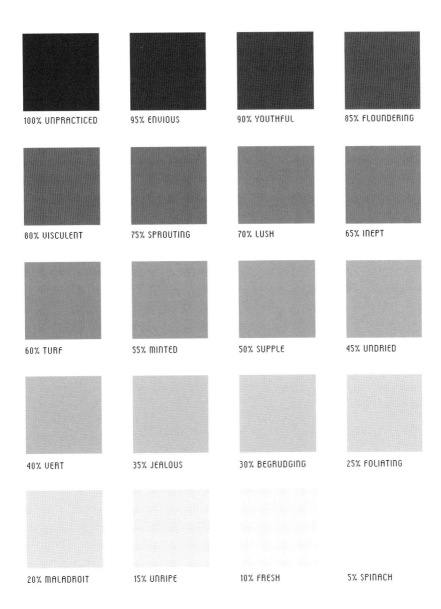

100% UNPRACTICED   95% ENVIOUS   90% YOUTHFUL   85% FLOUNDERING

80% VISCULENT   75% SPROUTING   70% LUSH   65% INEPT

60% TURF   55% MINTED   50% SUPPLE   45% UNDRIED

40% VERT   35% JEALOUS   30% BEGRUDGING   25% FOLIATING

20% MALADROIT   15% UNRIPE   10% FRESH   5% SPINACH

FREE?FONTS SWATCH

Duality

abcdefghijklmnopqrstuvwxyz
ABCDEFGHIJKLMNOPQRSTUVWXYZ
0123456789 (..;:?!$&-*) @"#%'+/\<>=_ `€

Weights Available: Regular

Designer: Ray Larabie

Website: www.larabiefonts.com

Platform: PC, Mac

Category: Decorative, Display

Date of Creation: 2000

Additional Information: Other freeware & shareware fonts are available from the same source and commercial fonts are available from the same designer at www.typodermic.com.

Read Me: This font is free to use for personal and/or commercial purposes. No payment is necessary but a sample of your product would be gratefully appreciated so I can see how the font looks in use.

If you'd like to make a voluntary donation to Larabie Fonts for the use of the free fonts in any amount please go to www.larabiefonts.com/donation.html.

Some Larabie fonts have enhanced and expanded families available for sale at: www.typodermic.com.

NB: A complete licence agreement is enclosed with each 'Larabie' font downloaded.

Direct URL: www.myfonts.com/fonts/larabie/duality/

Euphoria

Lose your memory

Lose your mind

Tell all

Throw a seven

Walk out

DustDot

abcdefghijklmnopqrstuvwxyz
ABCDEFGHIJKLMNOPQRSTUVWXYZ
0123456789 (.,;:?!$&—*) ‹@"#%'+/\[<>=]^_`|"›

Weights Available: Regular

Designer: Hiroshi Kuzumi

Website: www.kuzumi.net

Platform: PC, Mac

Category: Pixel

Date of Creation: 2004

Additional Information: Other freeware & shareware fonts are available from the same source. Please visit the designer's website.

Read Me: This font is freeware. You can use it on anything you like!

Direct URL: www.kuzumi.net/main.html

abcdefghijklmnopqrstuvwxyz
ABCDEFGHIJKLMNOPQRSTUVWXYZ
0123456789 (.,;:?!$&-*) {@"#%'+/\[<>=]^'|~}

Weights Available: **Medium**

Designer: Hiroshi Kuzumi

Website: www.kuzumi.net

Platform: PC, Mac

Category: Sans Serif

Date of Creation: 2002

Additional Information: Other freeware & shareware fonts are available from the same source. Please visit the designer's website.

Read Me: This font is freeware. You can use it on anything you like!

Direct URL: www.kuzumi.net/main.html

Echelon

abcdefghijklmnopqrstuvwxyz
ABCDEFGHIJKLMNOPQRSTUVWXYZ
0123456789 (.,::?!$&-*) {@"#%'+/\[<>=]^_ |€}

Weights Available: Regular, *Italic*

Designer: Ray Larabie	**Date of Creation:** 1999
Website: www.larabiefonts.com	**Additional Information:** Other freeware & shareware fonts are available from the same source and commercial fonts are available from the same designer at www.typodermic.com.
Platform: PC, Mac	
Category: Decorative	

Read Me: This font is free to use for personal and/or commercial purposes. No payment is necessary but a sample of your product would be gratefully appreciated so I can see how the font looks in use.

If you'd like to make a voluntary donation to Larabie Fonts for the use of the free fonts in any amount please go to www.larabiefonts.com/donation.html.

Some Larabie fonts have enhanced and expanded families available for sale at: www.typodermic.com.

NB: A complete licence agreement is enclosed with each 'Larabie' font downloaded.

Direct URL: www.myfonts.com/fonts/larabie/echelon/

Starter

Soft Potato Herb Gnocchi with Cep Sauce & Parmesan

Feta Cheese Salad, Garlic Stuffed Olives
Green Beans, & Fresh Peas with Salsa Verde

✕✖✕

Main

Risotto with Baked Cherry Tomatoes, Wild Garlic, Herbs & Parmesan

Breaded Aubergine stuffed with Smoked Mozzarella,
Romesco Sauce & Green Beans

✕✖✕

Dessert

Caramelised Banana Tart with Crème Fraîche

Rum Baba with Tropical Fruits, & Coconut Cream

✕✖✕

Tea or Coffee

After Dinner Chocolates

Effloresce

abcdefghijklmnopqrstuvwxyz
ABCDEFGHIJKLMNOPQRSTUVWXYZ
0123456789 [.,:;?!$&-*] {@"#%'+/\[<>=]^_`|}

Weights Available: Regular, *Italic,* **Bold,** *Bold italic*

Designer: Ray Larabie

Website: www.larabiefonts.com

Platform: PC, Mac

Category: Serif, Venetian

Date of Creation: 1999

Additional Information: Other freeware & shareware fonts are available from the same source and commercial fonts are available from the same designer at www.typodermic.com.

Read Me: This font is free to use for personal and/or commercial purposes. No payment is necessary but a sample of your product would be gratefully appreciated so I can see how the font looks in use.

If you'd like to make a voluntary donation to Larabie Fonts for the use of the free fonts in any amount please go to www.larabiefonts.com/donation.html.

Some Larabie fonts have enhanced and expanded families available for sale at: www.typodermic.com.

NB: A complete licence agreement is enclosed with each 'Larabie' font downloaded.

Direct URL: www.myfonts.com/fonts/larabie/effloresce/

abcdefghijklmnopqrstuvwxyz
ABCDEFGHIJKLMNOPQRSTUVWXYZ
0123456789 (.,;:?!$&-*) @"#%'+/< > =_`\€

Weights Available: Regular

Designer: Ray Larabie

Website: www.larabiefonts.com

Platform: PC, Mac

Category: Decorative

Date of Creation: 1999

Additional Information: Other freeware & shareware fonts are available from the same source and commercial fonts are available from the same designer at www.typodermic.com.

Read Me: This font is free to use for personal and/or commercial purposes. No payment is necessary but a sample of your product would be gratefully appreciated so I can see how the font looks in use.

If you'd like to make a voluntary donation to Larabie Fonts for the use of the free fonts in any amount please go to www.larabiefonts.com/donation.html.

Some Larabie fonts have enhanced and expanded families available for sale at: www.typodermic.com.

NB: A complete licence agreement is enclosed with each 'Larabie' font downloaded.

Direct URL: www.myfonts.com/fonts/larabie/euphorigenic/

Forgotten Futurist

abcdefghijklmnopqrstuvwxyz
ABCDEFGHIJKLMNOPQRSTUVWXYZ
0123456789 (.,;:?!$&-*) ◄@"#%'+/\[<>=]^_`| €►

Weights Available: Regular, *Italic*, **Bold**, ***Bold italic***   **Family:** Shadow

Designer: Ray Larabie

Website: www.larabiefonts.com

Platform: PC, Mac

Category: Sans Serif

Date of Creation: 1999

Additional Information: Other freeware & shareware fonts are available from the same source and commercial fonts are available from the same designer at www.typodermic.com.

Read Me: This font is free to use for personal and/or commercial purposes. No payment is necessary but a sample of your product would be gratefully appreciated so I can see how the font looks in use.

If you'd like to make a voluntary donation to Larabie Fonts for the use of the free fonts in any amount please go to www.larabiefonts.com/donation.html.

Some Larabie fonts have enhanced and expanded families available for sale at: www.typodermic.com.

NB: A complete licence agreement is enclosed with each 'Larabie' font downloaded.

Direct URL: www.myfonts.com/fonts/larabie/forgotten-futurist/

Thy word is a lamp unto my feet, and a light unto my path. Psalm 119:105

FT Rosecube

ABCDEFGHIJKLMNOPQRSTUVWXYZ
ABCDEFGHIJKLMNOPQRSTUVWXYZ
0123456789 (.,;:?!&-) ''%'/

Weights Available: NORMAL

Designer: Emil Bertell	Date of Creation: 2005
Website: www.fenotype.com	Additional Information: Other freeware, shareware and commercial fonts are available from the same source.
Platform: PC, Mac	
Category: 3D	Please visit the designer's website.

NB: There is no Read Me file accompanying this font, however, please respect the designer's rights. If there are any queries as to how this font can be used please contact the designer directly.

Direct URL: www.fenotype.com/font/fontpage.htm

ABCDEFGHIJKLMNOPQRSTUVWXYZ
ABCDEFGHIJKLMNOPQRSTUVWXYZ
0123456789 (.,:?!$&-*) -+- "%'+/\=_£

Weights Available: REGULAR

Designer: Damien Gosset

Website: www.daaams.fr.st

Platform: PC, Mac

Category: Trash

Date of Creation: Information not provided

Additional Information: Other freeware, shareware and commercial fonts are available from the same source.

Please visit the designer's website.

Read Me: This is a 'Drinkware' font, it can be used for free for your personal use only, and if you're nice you can send me a bottle of local beer (and don't hesitate to send me samples of your work, made with this font).

A Read Me file accompanies this font, always keep these files together.

If you want to use Fucked Plate for commercial purposes, please drop me an e-mail.

Direct URL: www.dafont.com/font.php?file=fucked_plate

Guilty

abcdefghijklmnopqrstuvwxyz
abcdefghijklmnopqrstuvwxyz
0123456789 (.,;:?!$&-*) {@"#%'+/\[<>=]^_'|~tt}

Weights Available: regular

Designer: Eduardo Recife

Website: www.misprintedtype.com

Platform: PC, Mac

Category: Grunge, Display

Date of Creation: 1998-2004

Additional Information: Other freeware &
shareware fonts are available from the same
source. Please visit the designer's website.

Read Me: This is a freeware typeface and can be used on your commercial or non-commercial
work for free. But here is a list of things you could do, only if you want to:

Link www.misprintedtype.com on your site, send me a sample of the work you did using my
typeface, mail me some printed material using my typeface, credit 'misprinted type' on your
work, donate money, books, cds, artwork, whatever you want.

DO NOT: Sell this font or modify it.

DO NOT: Redistribute this font without my permission.

Direct URL: www.misprintedtype.com/v3/fonts.php

abcdefghijklmnopqrstuvwxyz
ABCDEFGHIJKLMNOPQRSTUVWXYZ
0123456789 (.,:?!$€-*) {@"#%/\[]^_`|~€}

Weights Available: Regular

Designer: Amy E. Conger

Website: www.abecedarienne.com

Platform PC, Mac

Category: Hand lettered

Date of Creation: 2004

Additional Information: Other freeware & shareware fonts are available from the same source. Please visit the designer's website.

Read Me: You may distribute this font shamelessly. You may translate it to any platform, just don't change the name. You may remix it, just give me credit and let me know.

Direct URL: www.abecedarienne.com/index.shtml#halcyon

Hayes

abcdefghijklmnopqrstuvwxyz
ABCDEFGHIJKLMNOPQRSTUVWXYZ
0123456789 (.,:?!$+-*) <@"#%'+/\[<>=]^_¦~>

Weights Available: Justice

Designer: Kent Hertzog

Website: www.digitallybranded.com

Platform: PC, Mac

Category: Pixel

Date of Creation: 2004

Additional Information: Other freeware & shareware fonts are available from the same source. Please visit the designer's website.

NB: There is no Read Me file accompanying this font, however, all Digitally Branded fonts are fully freeware. Do not sell or modify the font and please respect the designer's rights. If there are any queries as to how this font can be used please contact the designer directly.

Direct URL: www.digitallybranded.com/v3/v3.html

abcdefghijklmnopqrstuvwxyz
ABCDEFGHIJKLMNOPQRSTUVWXYZ
0123456789 (.,:;?!$+-*) {@"#%'+/\[<>=]^_`|~}

Weights Available: **Justice**

Designer: Kent Hertzog

Website: www.digitallybranded.com

Platform: PC, Mac

Category: Pixel

Date of Creation: 2002

Additional Information: Other freeware & shareware fonts are available from the same source. Please visit the designer's website.

NB: There is no Read Me file accompanying this font, however, all Digitally Branded fonts are fully freeware. Do not sell or modify the font and please respect the designer's rights. If there are any queries as to how this font can be used please contact the designer directly.

Direct URL: www.digitallybranded.com/v3/v3.html

Hearst

abcdefghijklmnopqrstuvwxyz
ABCDEFGHIJKLMNOPQRSTUVWXYZ
0123456789 (.,;:?!$+-*) (@"#%'+/\[<>=]^_`|~)

Weights Available: Justice

Designer: Kent Hertzog

Website: www.digitallybranded.com

Platform: PC, Mac

Category: Pixel

Date of Creation: 2004

Additional Information: Other freeware & shareware fonts are available from the same source. Please visit the designer's website.

NB: There is no Read Me file accompanying this font, however, all Digitally Branded fonts are fully freeware. Do not sell or modify the font and please respect the designer's rights. If there are any queries as to how this font can be used please contact the designer directly.

Direct URL: www.digitallybranded.com/v3/v3.html

Heimchen (Das Gute)

abcdefgh ijklmnopqrstuvwxyz

ABcDEFcHIJKLMnOPpRSTVvWXYz

0123456789 . ,; ¡ !-'+/=

Weights Available: **No Mix'sch**

Designer: Boris Moser

Website: www.helldunkel.com

Platform: PC

Category: Grunge

Date of Creation: 2005

Additional Information: Other freeware & shareware fonts are available from the same source. Please visit the designer's website.

Read Me: All helldunkel.com fonts are freeware. You can do whatever the heck you want to do with them – which includes for private or commercial use, just enjoy.

Direct URL: www.helldunkel.com/2005/set.htm

Horse Puke

abcdefghijklmnopqrstuvwxyz
ABCDEFGHIJKLMNOPQRSTUVWXYZ
0123456789 (.,:?!$&-') [@"#%'^\<>=]'_`|~Ð]

Weights Available: Regular

Designer: Eduardo Recife

Website: www.misprintedtype.com

Platform: PC, Mac

Category: Grunge, Display

Date of Creation: 1998-2004

Additional Information: Other freeware & shareware fonts are available from the same source. Please visit the designer's website.

Read Me: This is a freeware typeface and can be used on your commercial or non-commercial work for free. But here is a list of things you could do, only if you want to:

Link www.misprintedtype.com on your site, send me a sample of the work you did using my typeface, mail me some printed material using my typeface, credit misprinted type' on your work, donate money, books, cds, artwork, whatever you want.

DO NOT: Sell this font or modify it.

DO NOT: Redistribute this font without my permission.

Direct URL: www.misprintedtype.com/v3/fonts.php

ABSOLUTELY
NO PARKING

Hurry Up

ABCDEFGHIJKLMNOPQRSTUVWXYZ
ABCDEFGHIJKLMNOPQRSTUVWXYZ
0123456789 (.,:;?$&-*) {@"#%'+ /\[←→=]A_ `|€}

Weights Available: REGULAR

Designer: Ray Larabie

Website: www.larabiefonts.com

Platform: PC, Mac

Category: Decorative, Funny

Date of Creation: 1998

Additional Information: Other freeware & shareware fonts are available from the same source and commercial fonts are available from the same designer at www.typodermic.com.

Read Me: This font is free to use for personal and/or commercial purposes. No payment is necessary but a sample of your product would be gratefully appreciated so I can see how the font looks in use.

If you'd like to make a voluntary donation to Larabie Fonts for the use of the free fonts in any amount please go to www.larabiefonts.com/donation.html.

Some Larabie fonts have enhanced and expanded families available for sale at: www.typodermic.com.

NB: A complete licence agreement is enclosed with each 'Larabie' font downloaded.

Direct URL: www.myfonts.com/fonts/larabie/hurry-up/

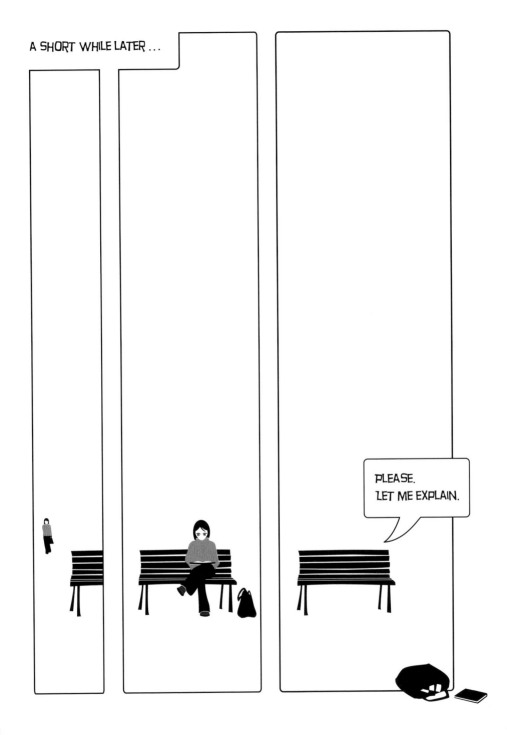

Interplanetary Crap

abcdefghijklmnopqrstuvwxyz
ABCDEFGHIJKLMNOPQRSTUVWXYZ
0123456789 (.,;:?!$&-*) ©"#%'+/\<>=^_`|

Weights Available: Regular

Designer: Ray Larabie

Website: www.larabiefonts.com

Platform: PC, Mac

Category: Stencil

Date of Creation: 1998

Additional Information: Other freeware & shareware fonts are available from the same source and commercial fonts are available from the same designer at www.typodermic.com.

Read Me: This font is free to use for personal and/or commercial purposes. No payment is necessary but a sample of your product would be gratefully appreciated so I can see how the font looks in use.

If you'd like to make a voluntary donation to Larabie Fonts for the use of the free fonts in any amount please go to www.larabiefonts.com/donation.html.

Some Larabie fonts have enhanced and expanded families available for sale at: www.typodermic.com.

NB: A complete licence agreement is enclosed with each 'Larabie' font downloaded.

Direct URL: www.myfonts.com/fonts/larabie/interplanetary-crap/

abcdefghijklmnopqrstuvwxyz
ABCDEFGHIJKLMNOPQRSTUVWXYZ
0123456789 (.,;:?!$&*) @"#%'/\x

Weights Available: Jack's Mannequin Regular, Jack's Mannequin Too Regular

---

Designer: Kent Hertzog

Website: www.digitallybranded.com

Platform: PC, Mac

Category: Hand written

Date of Creation: 2005

Additional Information: Other freeware & shareware fonts are available from the same source. Please visit the designer's website.

NB: There is no Read Me file accompanying this font, however, all Digitally Branded fonts are fully freeware. Do not sell or modify the font and please respect the designer's rights. If there are any queries as to how this font can be used please contact the designer directly.

Direct URL: www.digitallybranded.com/v3/v3.html

Kenyan Coffee

abcdefghijklmnopqrstuvwxyz
ABCDEFGHIJKLMNOPQRSTUVWXYZ
0123456789 (.,;:?!$&-*) {@"#%'+/\[‹›:]ˆ ` |€}

Weights Available: Regular, *Italic*, **Bold**, ***Bold italic***

Designer: Ray Larabie

Website: www.larabiefonts.com

Platform: PC, Mac

Category: Sans Serif

Date of Creation: 1999

Additional Information: Other freeware & shareware fonts are available from the same source and commercial fonts are available from the same designer at www.typodermic.com.

Read Me: This font is free to use for personal and/or commercial purposes. No payment is necessary but a sample of your product would be gratefully appreciated so I can see how the font looks in use.

If you'd like to make a voluntary donation to Larabie Fonts for the use of the free fonts in any amount please go to www.larabiefonts.com/donation.html.

Some Larabie fonts have enhanced and expanded families available for sale at: www.typodermic.com.

NB: A complete licence agreement is enclosed with each 'Larabie' font downloaded.

Direct URL: www.myfonts.com/fonts/larabie/kenyan-coffee/

Komodore

ABCDEFGHIJKLMNOPQRSTUVWXYZ
ABCDEFGHIJKLMNOPQRSTUVWXYZ
0123456789 (.,;:?!-×) (@"'+/\[()=]^_`|)

Weights Available: **NORMAL, DESTROY**

Designer: Nina David

Website: www.font-o-rama.com

Platform: PC, Mac

Category: Pixel

Date of Creation: 2000

Additional Information: Other freeware, shareware and commercial fonts are available from the same source.

Please visit the designer's website.

Read Me: This typeface is for free and meant 'as is'. You can copy and give it away to your friends as long as this Read Me file is included with the postscript data.

Don't try to distribute it!

Direct URL: www.font-o-rama.com/free_fonts/komodore.html

Libel Suit

abcdefghijklmnopqrstuvwxyz
ABCDEFGHIJKLMNOPQRSTUVWXYZ
0123456789 (.,:;?!$&-*) @"#%'+/\←<>=→^_`

Weights Available: Regular

Designer: Ray Larabie	Date of Creation: 1999
Website: www.larabiefonts.com	Additional Information: Other freeware & shareware fonts are available from the same source and commercial fonts are available from the same designer at www.typodermic.com.
Platform: PC, Mac	
Category: Sans Serif	

Read Me: This font is free to use for personal and/or commercial purposes. No payment is necessary but a sample of your product would be gratefully appreciated so I can see how the font looks in use.

If you'd like to make a voluntary donation to Larabie Fonts for the use of the free fonts in any amount please go to www.larabiefonts.com/donation.html.

Some Larabie fonts have enhanced and expanded families available for sale at: www.typodermic.com.

NB: A complete licence agreement is enclosed with each 'Larabie' font downloaded.

Direct URL: www.myfonts.com/fonts/larabie/libel-suit/

ABCDEF GHIJKL-MNOPQRSTUVWXYZ
ABCDEFGHIJKLMNoPQRSTUVWXYZ
0123456789 (.,:;?!$&—*) {@"#/+/\[<>=]^_|~}

Weights Available: REGULAR

Designer: Eduardo Recife

Website: www.misprintedtype.com

Platform: PC, Mac

Category: Grunge, Display

Date of Creation: 1998-2004

Additional Information: Other freeware & shareware fonts are available from the same source. Please visit the designer's website.

Read Me: This is a freeware typeface and can be used on your commercial or non-commercial work for free. But here is a list of things you could do, only if you want to:

Link www.misprintedtype.com on your site, send me a sample of the work you did using my typeface, mail me some printed material using my typeface, credit 'misprinted type' on your work, donate money, books, cds, artwork, whatever you want.

DO NOT: Sell this font or modify it.

DO NOT: Redistribute this font without my permission.

Direct URL: www.misprintedtype.com/v3/fonts.php

Memory Lapses

ABCDEFGHIJKLMNOPQRSTUVWXYZ
ABCDEFGHIJKLMNOPQRSTU VWXYZ
0123456789 (.,;:?!$&-·] @"#%'+/\'·'=:'_']

Weights Available: REGULAR

Designer: Eduardo Recife

Website: www.misprintedtype.com

Platform: PC, Mac

Category: Grunge, Display

Date of Creation: 1998-2004

Additional Information: Other freeware &
shareware fonts are available from the same
source. Please visit the designer's website.

Read Me: This is a freeware typeface and can be used on your commercial or non-commercial
work for free. But here is a list of things you could do, only if you want to:

Link www.misprintedtype.com on your site, send me a sample of the work you did using my
typeface, mail me some printed material using my typeface, credit 'misprinted type' on your
work, donate money, books, cds, artwork, whatever you want.

DO NOT: Sell this font or modify it.

DO NOT: Redistribute this font without my permission.

Direct URL: www.misprintedtype.com/v3/fonts.php

ABCDEFGHIJKLMNOPQRSTUVWXYZ
ABCDEFGHIJKLMNOPQRSTUVWXYZ
0123456789 (.,:?!$§-*) @"#%'+/\[<>=]^_ ID

Weights Available: REGULAR

Designer: Eduardo Recife

Website: www.misprintedtype.com

Platform: PC, Mac

Category: Grunge, Display

Date of Creation: 1998-2004

Additional Information: Other freeware & shareware fonts are available from the same source. Please visit the designer's website.

Read Me: This is a freeware typeface and can be used on your commercial or non-commercial work for free. But here is a list of things you could do, only if you want to:

Link www.misprintedtype.com on your site, send me a sample of the work you did using my typeface, mail me some printed material using my typeface, credit 'misprinted type' on your work, donate money, books, cds, artwork, whatever you want.

DO NOT: Sell this font or modify it.

DO NOT: Redistribute this font without my permission.

Direct URL: www.misprintedtype.com/v3/fonts.php

Motherfunker

ABCDEFGHIJKLMNOPQRSTUVWXYZ
ABCDEFGHIJKLMNOPQRSTUVWXYZ
0123456789.,;:?!+/

Weights Available: Regular

Designer: Boris Moser	Date of Creation: 2005
Website: www.helldunkel.com	Additional Information: Other freeware & shareware fonts are available from the same source. Please visit the designer's website.
Platform: PC	
Category: Grunge	

Read Me: All helldunkel.com fonts are freeware. You can do whatever the heck you want to do with them – which includes for private or commercial use, just enjoy.

Direct URL: www.helldunkel.com/2005/set.htm

Mulder handwriting

abcdefghijklmnopqrstuvwxyz
ABCDEFGHIJKLMNOPQRSTUVWXYZ
0123456789 (-,;:?!\$&-*) {@"#% '+ \[<>=]^_`|~}

Weights Available: Regular

Designer: Merijn C. Mulder

Website: www.studio37.nl

Platform: PC

Category: Hand written

Date of Creation: 2004

Additional Information: Other freeware & shareware fonts are available from the same source. Please visit the designer's website.

NB: There is no Read Me file accompanying this font, however, please respect the designer's rights. If there are any queries as to how this font can be used please contact the designer directly.

Direct URL: www.studio37.nl/mulder_hw.zip

Nail Scratch

ABCDEFGHIJKLMNOPQRSTUVWXYZ
ABCDEFGHIJKLMNOPQRSTUVWXYZ
0123456789 (.,:;?!$¢-*) /@"#%+/\[<>=]^_'|®—

Weights Available: REGULAR

Designer: Eduardo Recife

Website: www.misprintedtype.com

Platform: PC, Mac

Category: Grunge, Display

Date of Creation: 1998-2004

Additional Information: Other freeware & shareware fonts are available from the same source. Please visit the designer's website.

Read Me: This is a freeware typeface and can be used on your commercial or non-commercial work for free. But here is a list of things you could do, only if you want to:

Link www.misprintedtype.com on your site, send me a sample of the work you did using my typeface, mail me some printed material using my typeface, credit 'misprinted type' on your work, donate money, books, cds, artwork, whatever you want.

DO NOT: Sell this font or modify it.

DO NOT: Redistribute this font without my permission.

Direct URL: www.misprintedtype.com/v3/fonts.php

ABCDEFGHIJKLMNOPQRSTUVWXYZ
ABCDEFGHIJKLMNOPQRSTUVWXYZ
0123456789 (.,::?!§&-*) {@"#%'+/\[<>=]^_` |~D)

Weights Available: REGULAR

Designer: Eduardo Recife

Website: www.misprintedtype.com

Platform: PC, Mac

Category: Display

Date of Creation: 1998-2004

Additional Information: Remix from 'Extra Ornamental' by House of Lime.

Other freeware & shareware fonts are available from the same source. Please visit the designer's website.

Read Me: This is a freeware typeface and can be used on your commercial or non-commercial work for free. But here is a list of things you could do, only if you want to:

Link www.misprintedtype.com on your site, send me a sample of the work you did using my typeface, mail me some printed material using my typeface, credit 'misprinted type' on your work, donate money, books, cds, artwork, whatever you want.

DO NOT: Sell this font or modify it.

DO NOT: Redistribute this font without my permission.

Direct URL: www.misprintedtype.com/v3/fonts.php

Neasden PIP

ABCDEFGHIJKLMNOPQRSTUVWXYZ
ABCDEFGHIJKLMNOPQRSTUVWXYZ
0123456789 (.,;?!$ -*) @"#%'+/\[<>=]^_|~Ð

Font Family: NEASDEN PIP REGULAR, MISPRINTED PIP REGULAR

Designer: Steve Smith /Eduardo Recife

Website: See Additional Info

Platform: PC, Mac

Category: Grunge, Display

Date of Creation: 1998-2004

Additional Information: This type was designed as a collaboration between Neasden Control Centre: www.neasdencontrol.com and Misprinted Type: www.misprintedtype.com

Read Me: This is a freeware typeface and can be used on your commercial or non-commercial work for free. But here is a list of things you could do, only if you want to:

Link www.misprintedtype.com on your site, send me a sample of the work you did using my typeface, mail me some printed material using my typeface, credit 'misprinted type' on your work, donate money, books, cds, artwork, whatever you want.

DO NOT: Sell this font or modify it.

DO NOT: Redistribute this font without my permission.

Direct URL: www.misprintedtype.com/v3/fonts.php

abcdefghijklmnopqrstuvwxyz
ABCDEFGHIJKLMNOPQRSTUVWXYZ
0123456789 (.,;:?!¥&-*) («"#%'÷/♀♦♥♣≈♦♦♦)

Weights Available: *Regular*

Designer: Joseph Sinel	Date of Creation: 2000
Website: www.p22.com	Additional Information: The free font includes the basic character set plus ornaments.
Platform: PC, Mac	Other freeware, shareware & commercial fonts
Category: Art Deco Display	are available from the same source.

Read Me: This font is offered for free and available only from P22's website. As a free font, no technical support can be offered and no claims are made as to the fitness of this font for any given situation. It can be used for personal projects and commercial products up to 1,000 pieces.

For commercial products over 1,000 pieces, a licensing fee will be required.

The standard P22 licence agreement also applies to multiple users. One P22 font is licenced for up to 5 users on 1 output device. For a number of users and output devices which exceeds this, please call for site licence details.

P22 Sinel is available only from P22 Type Foundry. No other re-distribution in any way is allowed.

NB: A complete licence agreement is enclosed with each 'P22' font downloaded.

Direct URL: www.p22.com/products/freefont.html

P22 Typewriter

abcdefghijklmnopqrstuvwxyz
ABCDEFGHIJKLMNOPQRSTUVWXYZ
0123456789 (.,;:?!$&-*)
{@"#%'+/\[<>=]^_`|~Ð}

Weights Available: Regular

Designer: Richard Kegler

Website: www.p22.com

Platform: PC, Mac

Category: Text, Display

Date of Creation: 2001

Additional Information: Other freeware, shareware & commercial fonts are available from the same source. Please visit the designer's website for more information.

Read Me: This font is offered for free and available only from P22's website. As a free font, no technical support can be offered and no claims are made as to the fitness of this font for any given situation. It can be used for personal projects and commercial products up to 1,000 pieces.

For commercial products over 1,000 pieces, a licensing fee will be required.

The standard P22 licence agreement also applies to multiple users. One P22 font is licenced for up to 5 users on 1 output device. For a number of users and output devices which exceeds this, please call for site licence details.

P22 Typewriter is available only from P22 Type Foundry. No other re-distribution in any way is allowed.

NB: A complete licence agreement is enclosed with each 'P22' font downloaded.

Direct URL: www.p22.com/products/freefont.html

Miss Vetz,

·der to make your new insoles, we require
shoe size. Would you please contact us on Tel-
·8 to let us know your size.

: you.

·cal Appliances.

Pagra

ΛBCDEΓGhIJ⼊LMNOPORS⼅UVⱮXⳐZ
ΛBCDEΓGhIJ⼊LMNOPORS⼅UVⱮXⳐZ
C123⼂56⼅89 .,;:?!-=_

Weights Available: REGULAR

Designer: Nina David

Website: www.font-o-rama.com

Platform: PC, Mac

Category: Palm

Date of Creation: 2001

Additional Information: Other freeware, shareware and commercial fonts are available from the same source.

Please visit the designer's website.

Read Me: This typeface is for free and meant 'as is'. You can copy and give it away to your friends as long as this Read Me file is included with the postscript data.

Don't try to distribute it!

Direct URL: www.font-o-rama.com/free_fonts/pagra.html

Pastelaria

ABCDEFGHIJKLMNOPQRSTUVWXYZ
ABCDEFGHIJKLMNOPQRSTUVWXYZ
0123456789 [..::?!$¢-*] {@"#%'+/\[<>=]^_`|~0}

Weights Available: REGULAR

Designer: Eduardo Recife

Website: www.misprintedtype.com

Platform: PC, Mac

Category: Grunge, Display

Date of Creation: 1998-2004

Additional Information: Other freeware & shareware fonts are available from the same source. Please visit the designer's website.

Read Me: This is a freeware typeface and can be used on your commercial or non-commercial work for free. But here is a list of things you could do, only if you want to:

Link www.misprintedtype.com on your site, send me a sample of the work you did using my typeface, mail me some printed material using my typeface, credit 'misprinted type' on your work, donate money, books, cds, artwork, whatever you want.

DO NOT: Sell this font or modify it.

DO NOT: Redistribute this font without my permission.

Direct URL: www.misprintedtype.com/v3/fonts.php

ABCDEFGHIJKLMNOPQRSTUUWXYZ
ABCDEFGHIJKLMNOPQRSTUUWXYZ
0123456789 [.,;:?!-*) "'+/\(=)_|

Weights Available: LIGHT

Designer: Boris Moser

Website: www.helldunkel.com

Platform: PC

Category: Display

Date of Creation: 2005

Additional Information: Other freeware & shareware fonts are available from the same source. Please visit the designer's website.

Read Me: All helldunkel.com fonts are freeware. You can do whatever the heck you want to do with them – which includes for private or commercial use, just enjoy.

Direct URL: www.helldunkel.com/2005/set.htm

Perlon

abcdefghijklmnopqrstuvwxyz
ABCDEFGHIJKLMNOPQRSTUVWXYZ
0123456789[.,;:?!-*]""'+/<>=

Weights Available: fat

Designer: Boris Moser

Website: www.helldunkel.com

Platform: PC

Category: Grunge, Display

Date of Creation: 2005

Additional Information: Other freeware & shareware fonts are available from the same source. Please visit the designer's website.

Read Me: All helldunkel.com fonts are freeware. You can do whatever the heck you want to do with them – which includes for private or commercial use, just enjoy.

Direct URL: www.helldunkel.com/2005/set.htm

Porcelain

abcdefghijklmnopqrstuvwxyz
ABCDEFGHIJKLMNOPQRSTUVWXYZ
0123456789 (.,:;?!&-) {@"#%'+/\ ^` /~?}*

Weights Available: *Regular*

Designer: Eduardo Recife

Website: www.misprintedtype.com

Platform: PC, Mac

Category: Grunge, Display

Date of Creation: 1998-2004

Additional Information: Other freeware & shareware fonts are available from the same source. Please visit the designer's website.

Read Me: This is a freeware typeface and can be used on your commercial or non-commercial work for free. But here is a list of things you could do, only if you want to:

Link www.misprintedtype.com on your site, send me a sample of the work you did using my typeface, mail me some printed material using my typeface, credit 'misprinted type' on your work, donate money, books, cds, artwork, whatever you want.

DO NOT: Sell this font or modify it.

DO NOT: Redistribute this font without my permission.

Direct URL: www.misprintedtype.com/v3/fonts.php

abcdefghijklmnopqrstuvwxyz
ABCDEFGHIJKLMNOPQRSTUVWXYZ
0123456789 [.,;:?!$&-*] {@"#%'+/\[<>=]_` |~}

Weights Available: Regular

Designer:	Ray Larabie	Date of Creation:	1998

Website: www.larabiefonts.com

Platform: PC, Mac

Category: Sans Serif, Square

Additional Information: Other freeware & shareware fonts are available from the same source and commercial fonts are available from the same designer at www.typodermic.com.

Read Me: This font is free to use for personal and/or commercial purposes. No payment is necessary but a sample of your product would be gratefully appreciated so I can see how the font looks in use.

If you'd like to make a voluntary donation to Larabie Fonts for the use of the free fonts in any amount please go to www.larabiefonts.com/donation.html.

Some Larabie fonts have enhanced and expanded families available for sale at: www.typodermic.com.

NB: A complete licence agreement is enclosed with each 'Larabie' font downloaded.

Direct URL: www.myfonts.com/fonts/larabie/pricedown/

Prime Minister of Canada

ABCDEFGHIJKLMNOPQRSTUVWXYZ
ABCDEFGHIJKLMNOPQRSTUVWXYZ
0123456789 (.,;:?! $ & - *) ℗" #% '+ ∧= _`

Weights Available: REGULAR

Designer: Ray Larabie

Website: www.larabiefonts.com

Platform: PC, Mac

Category: Decorative

Date of Creation: 1997

Additional Information: Other freeware &
shareware fonts are available from the same
source and commercial fonts are available from
the same designer at www.typodermic.com.

Read Me: This font is free to use for personal and/or commercial purposes. No payment
is necessary but a sample of your product would be gratefully appreciated so I can see how
the font looks in use.

If you'd like to make a voluntary donation to Larabie Fonts for the use of the free fonts
in any amount please go to www.larabiefonts.com/donation.html.

Some Larabie fonts have enhanced and expanded families available for sale
at: www.typodermic.com.

NB: A complete licence agreement is enclosed with each 'Larabie' font downloaded.

Direct URL: www.myfonts.com/fonts/larabie/prime-minister-of-canada/

aBCDeFGHIJKLMNOPQrSTUVWXYZ
aBCDeFGHIJKLMNOPQrSTUVWXYZ
0123456789 (..,.:?!$&-*) {@"#%'+/\[<>=]^_`|€}

Weights Available: regular

Designer: Ray Larabie

Website: www.larabiefonts.com

Platform: PC, Mac

Category: Decorative

Date of Creation: 2001

Additional Information: Other freeware & shareware fonts are available from the same source and commercial fonts are available from the same designer at www.typodermic.com.

Read Me: This font is free to use for personal and/or commercial purposes. No payment is necessary but a sample of your product would be gratefully appreciated so I can see how the font looks in use.

If you'd like to make a voluntary donation to Larabie Fonts for the use of the free fonts in any amount please go to www.larabiefonts.com/donation.html.

Some Larabie fonts have enhanced and expanded families available for sale at: www.typodermic.com.

NB: A complete licence agreement is enclosed with each 'Larabie' font downloaded.

Direct URL: www.myfonts.com/fonts/larabie/pupcat/

Queen of Pain

abcdefghijklmnopqrstuvwxyz
ABCDEFGHIJKLMNOPQRSTUVWXYZ
0123456789 (.,;:?!$&-*) {@"#%'+/\[<>=]^_`|~}

Weights Available: Alk 3

Designer: Kent Hertzog

Website: www.digitallybranded.com

Platform: PC, Mac

Category: Ornate

Date of Creation: 2002

Additional Information: Other freeware & shareware fonts are available from the same source. Please visit the designer's website.

NB: There is no Read Me file accompanying this font, however, all Digitally Branded fonts are fully freeware. Do not sell or modify the font and please respect the designer's rights. If there are any queries as to how this font can be used please contact the designer directly.

Direct URL: www.digitallybranded.com/v3/v3.html

ABCDEFGHIJKLMNOPQRSTUVWXYZ
ABCDEFGHIJKLMNOPQRSTUVWXYZ
0123456789(. , ; : ? ! $&- ×)
{ @ " # % ' + / \ [< > =] _ | }

Weights Available: REGULAR

Designer: Nina David

Website: www.font-o-rama.com

Platform: PC, Mac

Category: Pixel

Date of Creation: 2003

Additional Information: Other freeware, shareware and commercial fonts are available from the same source.

Please visit the designer's website.

Read Me: This typeface is for free and meant 'as is'. You can copy and give it away to your friends as long as this Read Me file is included with the postscript data.

Don't try to distribute it!

Direct URL: www.font-o-rama.com/free_fonts/record.html

Respess Capitals

ABCDEFGHIJKLMNOPQRSTUVWXYZ
ABCDEFGHIJKLMNOPQRSTUVWXYZ
0123456789 .,:!$&~'""/

Weights Available: LIGHT, MEDIUM, **HEAVY, EXCESSIVE**

Designer: Amy E. Conger

Website: www.abecedarienne.com

Platform: PC, Mac

Category: Hand lettered

Date of Creation: 2003

Additional Information: Other freeware & shareware fonts are available from the same source. Please visit the designer's website.

Read Me: You may distribute this font shamelessly. You may translate it to any platform, just don't change the name. You may remix it, just give me credit and let me know.

Direct URL: www.abecedarienne.com/index.shtml#respess

SCORPIO

OCTOBER 24TH – NOVEMBER 22ND

SYMBOL: THE SCORPION

ELEMENT: WATER

BIRTHSTONE: TOPAZ

COLOUR: BLACK

RULING PLANETS: PLUTO AND MARS

BODY PARTS: GENITALS, REPRODUCTIVE ORGANS

COMMON TRAITS: SCORPIO IS THE MOST POWERFUL SIGN IN THE ZODIAC; BEING FORCEFUL, DETERMINED, DOMINANT, STRONG WILLED AND COURAGEOUS. SCORPIO IS ALSO KNOWN AS THE PASSIONATE SIGN OF THE ZODIAC, BEING SEXY AND MYSTERIOUS.

THE SCORPIO IS A DEEP THINKER WITH A FINE MIND, THEY ARE INTROSPECTIVE, TEMPERAMENTAL AND INTENSE. THEY ARE LOYAL, TENACIOUS, COMPULSIVE AND MAGNETIC. SCORPIOS OFTEN DEVELOP LOVE–HATE RELATIONSHIPS, PARTICULARLY WITH OTHER WATER SIGNS LIKE PISCES AND CANCER AND EARTH SIGNS LIKE CAPRICORN, TAURUS AND VIRGO.

POSSIBLE NEGATIVE TRAITS: SCORPIOS CAN BE VINDICTIVE, MOODY, SULLEN, BITTER, SARCASTIC POSSESSIVE AND JEALOUS. THEY ARE EXTREMELY UNPREDICTABLE AND HAVE A FIERY TEMPER. THEY MAY MISUSE SEX.

Rochester

abcdefghijklmnopqrstuvwxyz
ABCDEFGHIJKLMNOPQRSTUVWXYZ
0123456789:¢.,;;?!$&-*} @"#%'+/\[<>=]^_'|~Ð

Weights Available: Regular

Designer: Eduardo Recife	**Date of Creation:** 1998-2004
Website: www.misprintedtype.com	**Additional Information:** Other freeware & shareware fonts are available from the same source. Please visit the designer's website.
Platform: PC, Mac	
Category: Grunge, Display	

Read Me: This is a freeware typeface and can be used on your commercial or non-commercial work for free. But here is a list of things you could do, only if you want to:

Link www.misprintedtype.com on your site, send me a sample of the work you did using my typeface, mail me some printed material using my typeface, credit 'misprinted type' on your work, donate money, books, cds, artwork, whatever you want.

DO NOT: Sell this font or modify it.

DO NOT: Redistribute this font without my permission.

Direct URL: www.misprintedtype.com/v3/fonts.php

abcdefghijklmnopqrstuvwxyz

ABCDEFGHIJKLMNOPQRSTUVWXYZ

0123456789 (..:?!&-)¨#%·/|-^_`/~

Weights Available: *Regular*

Designer: Eduardo Recife

Website: www.misprintedtype.com

Platform: PC, Mac

Category: Grunge, Display

Date of Creation: 1998-2004

Additional Information: Other freeware & shareware fonts are available from the same source. Please visit the designer's website.

Read Me: This is a freeware typeface and can be used on your commercial or non-commercial work for free. But here is a list of things you could do, only if you want to:

Link www.misprintedtype.com on your site, send me a sample of the work you did using my typeface, mail me some printed material using my typeface, credit 'misprinted type' on your work, donate money, books, cds, artwork, whatever you want.

DO NOT: Sell this font or modify it.

DO NOT: Redistribute this font without my permission.

Direct URL: www.misprintedtype.com/v3/fonts.php

Sexsmith

abcdefghijklmnopqrstuvwxyz
ABCDEFGHIJKLMNOPQRSTUVWXYZ
0123456789 (.,;:?!$&-*) {@"#%'+/\[<>=]_`|~€}

Weights Available: Regular

Designer: Ray Larabie

Website: www.larabiefonts.com

Platform: PC, Mac

Category: Slab Serif

Date of Creation: 1999

Additional Information: Other freeware & shareware fonts are available from the same source and commercial fonts are available from the same designer at www.typodermic.com.

Read Me: This font is free to use for personal and/or commercial purposes. No payment is necessary but a sample of your product would be gratefully appreciated so I can see how the font looks in use.

If you'd like to make a voluntary donation to Larabie Fonts for the use of the free fonts in any amount please go to www.larabiefonts.com/donation.html.

Some Larabie fonts have enhanced and expanded families available for sale at: www.typodermic.com.

NB: A complete licence agreement is enclosed with each 'Larabie' font downloaded.

Direct URL: www.myfonts.com/fonts/larabie/sexsmith/

Shamools

Weights Available: Single weight

Designer: Jeroen Klaver

Website: www.shamfonts.com

Platform: Mac

Category: Pictorial

Date of Creation: 2003

Additional Information: Other freeware, shareware and commercial fonts are available from the same source.

Please visit the designer's website.

Read Me: Do not use for big time advertising campaigns.

Direct URL: www.shamfonts.com

Shortcut

ABCDEFGHIJKLMNOPQRSTUVWXYZ
ABCDEFGHIJKLMNOPQRSTUVWXYZ
0123456789 (.,;:?!$&-*) {@"#%'+/\[<>=]^_`|~Ð

Weights Available: REGULAR

Designer: Eduardo Recife

Website: www.misprintedtype.com

Platform: PC, Mac

Category: Grunge, Display

Date of Creation: 1998-2004

Additional Information: Other freeware & shareware fonts are available from the same source. Please visit the designer's website.

Read Me: This is a freeware typeface and can be used on your commercial or non-commercial work for free. But here is a list of things you could do, only if you want to:

Link www.misprintedtype.com on your site, send me a sample of the work you did using my typeface, mail me some printed material using my typeface, credit 'misprinted type' on your work, donate money, books, cds, artwork, whatever you want.

DO NOT: Sell this font or modify it.

DO NOT: Redistribute this font without my permission.

Direct URL: www.misprintedtype.com/v3/fonts.php

Space Age

ΛBCDEℲGHIJKLMNOPQRSTUVWXYZ

ΛBCDEℲGHIJKLMNOPQRSTUVWXYZ

0123456789 (.,;:?!$€-*)

SPΛCE @ "#%'+/\A<>=ʌ‸‿/\ΞSPΛCE

Weights Available: REGULAR

....

Designer: Justin Callaghan

Website: www.mickeyavenue.com

Platform: PC, OpenType

Category: Geometric Display

Date of Creation: 2002

Additional Information: The OpenType version of this font contains 75 Autoligs.

Other freeware & shareware fonts are available from the same source.

....

Read Me: This font is free for personal use. For all other uses please contact the designer directly. Please include [the] Space.txt file with any redistribution.

....

Direct URL: www.mickeyavenue.com/fonts/spaceage/

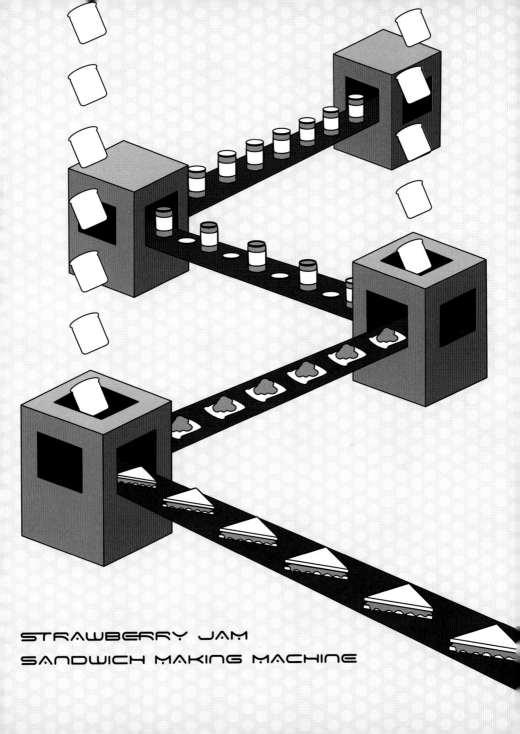

STRAWBERRY JAM
SANDWICH MAKING MACHINE

Splurge

abcdefghijklmnopqrstuvwxyz
ABCDEFGHIJKLMNOPQRSTUVWXYZ
0123456789 (.,;:?!$&-*) {@"#%'+/\[<>=]^_`|·}

Weights Available: Regular, **Bold**

Designer: Amy E. Conger	**Date of Creation:** 1994
Website: www.abecedarienne.com	**Additional Information:** Other freeware & shareware fonts are available from the same source. Please visit the designer's website.
Platform: PC, Mac	
Category: Hand lettered	

Read Me: You may distribute this font shamelessly. You may translate it to any platform, just don't change the name. You may remix it, just give me credit and let me know.

Direct URL: www.abecedarienne.com/index.shtml#splurge

ABCDEFGHIJKLMNOPQRSTUVWXYZ
ABCDEFGHIJKLMNOPQRSTUVWXYZ
0123456789 (..,::?!$&-*) {@"#%'+/\[<>=]^_|}

Weights Available: REGULAR

Designer: Ray Larabie

Website: www.larabiefonts.com

Platform: PC, Mac

Category: Sans Serif

Date of Creation: 2001

Additional Information: Other freeware & shareware fonts are available from the same source and commercial fonts are available from the same designer at www.typodermic.com.

Read Me: This font is free to use for personal and/or commercial purposes. No payment is necessary but a sample of your product would be gratefully appreciated so I can see how the font looks in use.

If you'd like to make a voluntary donation to Larabie Fonts for the use of the free fonts in any amount please go to www.larabiefonts.com/donation.html.

Some Larabie fonts have enhanced and expanded families available for sale at: www.typodermic.com.

NB: A complete licence agreement is enclosed with each 'Larabie' font downloaded.

Direct URL: www.myfonts.com/fonts/larabie/stentiga/

Street Cred

AbCdEFGHIJKLMNOPQRSTUVWXYZ
ABCDEFGHIJKLMNOPQRSTUVWXYZ
0123456789 [.,;:?!$£=✦] @"#%'⚡//\<>=_`

Weights Available: REGULAR

Designer: Ray Larabie

Website: www.larabiefonts.com

Platform: PC, Mac

Category: Decorative, Display

Date of Creation: 1998

Additional Information: Other freeware & shareware fonts are available from the same source and commercial fonts are available from the same designer at www.typodermic.com.

Read Me: This font is free to use for personal and/or commercial purposes. No payment is necessary but a sample of your product would be gratefully appreciated so I can see how the font looks in use.

If you'd like to make a voluntary donation to Larabie Fonts for the use of the free fonts in any amount please go to www.larabiefonts.com/donation.html.

Some Larabie fonts have enhanced and expanded families available for sale at: www.typodermic.com.

NB: A complete licence agreement is enclosed with each 'Larabie' font downloaded.

Direct URL: www.myfonts.com/fonts/larabie/street-cred/

Subamera

abcdefghijklmnopqrstuvwxyz
ABCDEFGHIJKLMNOPQRSTUVWXYZ
0123456789 (.,:;?!$&–*) {@"#%'+/\|<>=|^_`~€}

Weights Available: Regular

Designer: S. Théraulaz/V. Desrochers

Website: www.subtitude.com

Platform: PC, Mac

Category: Mechanical Trash

Date of Creation: 2005

Additional Information: Other freeware & shareware fonts are available from the same source. Please visit the designer's website.

Read Me: This font is not for resale. It is a shareware. You must always put a link to: www.subtitude.com if you offer this font for download. This font is not for commercial use, any resulting image(s) will remain the property of Subtitude Foundry. Legally, any adaptations are considered derivative works, and as such they remain the property of their inventor. Any character intended to be used as a trademark, logo and/or brand will first have to obtain a right of licence from Subtitude Foundry (www.subtitude.com).

NB: A complete licence agreement is enclosed with each 'Subtitude' font downloaded.

Direct URL: www.subtitude.com

Subelair

abcdeFGhiJKLMNOPQRStuVWXYZ

ABCDEFGHiJKLMNOPQRSTUVWXYZ

0123456789 (.,;:?!$&-*) {@"#%'+/\(<>=]_`|€}

Weights Available: **Regular**

Designer: Valérie Desrochers

Website: www.subtitude.com

Platform: PC, Mac

Category: Rounded Sans Serif

Date of Creation: 2006

Additional Information: Other freeware & shareware fonts are available from the same source. Please visit the designer's website.

Read Me: This font is not for resale. It is a shareware. You must always put a link to: www.subtitude.com if you offer this font for download. This font is not for commercial use, any resulting image(s) will remain the property of Subtitude Foundry. Legally, any adaptations are considered derivative works, and as such they remain the property of their inventor. Any character intended to be used as a trademark, logo and/or brand will first have to obtain a right of licence from Subtitude Foundry (www.subtitude.com).

NB: A complete licence agreement is enclosed with each 'Subtitude' font downloaded.

Direct URL: www.subtitude.com

Weights Available: Single weight

Designer: S. Théraulaz/V. Desrochers

Website: www.subtitude.com

Platform: PC, Mac

Category: Dingbat

Date of Creation: 2004

Additional Information: Other freeware & shareware fonts are available from the same source. Please visit the designer's website.

Read Me: This font is not for resale. It is a shareware. You must always put a link to: www.subtitude.com if you offer this font for download. This font is not for commercial use, any resulting image(s) will remain the property of Subtitude Foundry. Legally, any adaptations are considered derivative works, and as such they remain the property of their inventor. Any character intended to be used as a trademark, logo and/or brand will first have to obtain a right of licence from Subtitude Foundry (www.subtitude.com).

NB: A complete licence agreement is enclosed with each 'Subtitude' font downloaded.

Direct URL: www.subtitude.com

Suboel

Weights Available: Single weight

Designer: S. Théraulaz/V. Desrochers

Website: www.subtitude.com

Platform: PC, Mac

Category: Bitmap Symbols, Dingbat

Date of Creation: 2005

Additional Information: Other freeware & shareware fonts are available from the same source. Please visit the designer's website.

Read Me: This font is not for resale. It is a shareware. You must always put a link to: www.subtitude.com if you offer this font for download. This font is not for commercial use, any resulting image(s) will remain the property of Subtitude Foundry. Legally, any adaptations are considered derivative works, and as such they remain the property of their inventor. Any character intended to be used as a trademark, logo and/or brand will first have to obtain a right of licence from Subtitude Foundry (www.subtitude.com).

NB: A complete licence agreement is enclosed with each 'Subtitude' font downloaded.

Direct URL: www.subtitude.com

abCdEFGHIJKLMNOPQRSTUVWXYZ
aBCDEFGHIJKLMNOPQRSTUVWXYZ
0123456789 (.,;:?!$&-*) @"#%'+/\[<>=]_ ~€

Weights Available: REGULAR

Designer: Ray Larabie

Website: www.larabiefonts.com

Platform: PC, Mac

Category: Decorative, Display

Date of Creation: 2000

Additional Information: Other freeware & shareware fonts are available from the same source and commercial fonts are available from the same designer at www.typodermic.com.

Read Me: This font is free to use for personal and/or commercial purposes. No payment is necessary but a sample of your product would be gratefully appreciated so I can see how the font looks in use.

If you'd like to make a voluntary donation to Larabie Fonts for the use of the free fonts in any amount please go to www.larabiefonts.com/donation.html.

Some Larabie fonts have enhanced and expanded families available for sale at: www.typodermic.com.

NB: A complete licence agreement is enclosed with each 'Larabie' font downloaded.

Direct URL: www.myfonts.com/fonts/larabie/sybil-green/

The Time of the Revolving Door and Friends

abcdefghijklmnopqrstuvwxyz
ABCDEFGHIJKLMNOPQRSTUVWXYZ
0123456789 (.,:;?!$¢+~*) {@"#%+/\[<>=]‗}

Weights Available: Regular

Designer: Amy E. Conger

Website: www.abecedarienne.com

Platform: PC, Mac

Category: Hand lettered

Date of Creation: 2001

Additional Information: Other freeware & shareware fonts are available from the same source. Please visit the designer's website.

Read Me: You may distribute this font shamelessly. You may translate it to any platform, just don't change the name. You may remix it, just give me credit and let me know.

Direct URL: www.abecedarienne.com/index.shtml#revdoor

Mid-day / Mid-night

Eleven Oh Clock

One Oh Clock

Ten Oh Clock

Two Oh Clock

Nine Oh Clock

Three Oh Clock

Eight Oh Clock

Four Oh Clock

Seven Oh Clock

Five Oh Clock

Six Oh Clock

Thicket

abcdefghijklmnopqrstuvwxyz
ABCDEFGHIJKLMNOPQRSTUVWXYZ
0123456789 (.,;:?!$&-*) {@"#%'+/\[<>=]^_|}

Weights Available: Regular

Designer: Amy E. Conger	**Date of Creation:** 1994
Website: www.abecedarienne.com	**Additional Information:** Other freeware & shareware fonts are available from the same source. Please visit the designer's website.
Platform: PC, Mac	
Category: Hand lettered	

Read Me: You may distribute this font shamelessly. You may translate it to any platform, just don't change the name. You may remix it, just give me credit and let me know.

Direct URL: www.abecedarienne.com/index.shtml#thicket

Ooo Ohh

TicketCapitals

ABCDEFGHIJKLMNOPQRSTUVWXYZ
ABCDEFGHIJKLMNOPQRSTUVWXYZ
0123456789 .,;:?!$& /\

Weights Available: IMPRESSED, REPRESSED

Designer: Amy E. Conger

Website: www.abecedarienne.com

Platform: PC, Mac

Category: Rubber Stamp

Date of Creation: 1994

Additional Information: Other freeware & shareware fonts are available from the same source. Please visit the designer's website.

Read Me: You may distribute this font shamelessly. You may translate it to any platform, just don't change the name. You may remix it, just give me credit and let me know.

Direct URL: www.abecedarienne.com/index.shtml#ticket

ABCDEFGHIJKLMNOPQRSTUVWXYZ
ABCDEFGHIJKLMNOPQRSTUVWXYZ
0123456789 (.,;:?!$&-*) {@"#%'+/\[<>=]^_`|~}

Weights Available: xmas

Designer: Nina David

Website: www.font-o-rama.com

Platform: PC, Mac

Category: Modern Sans Serif

Date of Creation: 2001

Additional Information: Other freeware & shareware and commercial fonts are available from the same source. Please visit the designer's website for more information.

Read Me: This typeface is for free and meant 'as is'. You can copy and give it away to your friends as long as this Read Me file is included with the postscript data.

Don't try to distribute it!

Direct URL: www.font-o-rama.com/free_fonts/unif_xmas.html

Velvenda Cooler

abcdefghijklmnopqrstuvwxyz
ABCDEFGHIJKLMNOPQRSTUVWXYZ
0123456789 [.,;:?!$¢-*] {@"#%'·/\[◊:]^` |£}

Font Family: VELVENDA COOLER REGULAR, VELVENDA MEGABLACK REGULAR

Designer: Ray Larabie

Website: www.larabiefonts.com

Platform: PC, Mac

Category: Decorative

Date of Creation: 2002

Additional Information: Other freeware & shareware fonts are available from the same source and commercial fonts are available from the same designer at www.typodermic.com.

Read Me: This font is free to use for personal and/or commercial purposes. No payment is necessary but a sample of your product would be gratefully appreciated so I can see how the font looks in use.

If you'd like to make a voluntary donation to Larabie Fonts for the use of the free fonts in any amount please go to www.larabiefonts.com/donation.html.

Some Larabie fonts have enhanced and expanded families available for sale at: www.typodermic.com.

NB: A complete licence agreement is enclosed with each 'Larabie' font downloaded.

Direct URL: www.myfonts.com/fonts/larabie/velvenda/

You're Gone

A3CDEFGHIJKLMNOPQRSTUVWXYZ
A3CDEFGHIJKLMNOPQRSTUVWXYZ
0123456789 (.,;:?!$&-*) @"#%'+/<>= ` ~€

Weights Available: REGULAR, ITALIC

Designer: Ray Larabie

Website: www.larabiefonts.com

Platform: PC, Mac

Category: Decorative, Sans Serif

Date of Creation: 2000

Additional Information: Other freeware & shareware fonts are available from the same source and commercial fonts are available from the same designer at www.typodermic.com.

Read Me: This font is free to use for personal and/or commercial purposes. No payment is necessary but a sample of your product would be gratefully appreciated so I can see how the font looks in use.

If you'd like to make a voluntary donation to Larabie Fonts for the use of the free fonts in any amount please go to www.larabiefonts.com/donation.html.

Some Larabie fonts have enhanced and expanded families available for sale at: www.typodermic.com.

NB: A complete licence agreement is enclosed with each 'Larabie' font downloaded.

Direct URL: www.myfonts.com/fonts/larabie/youre-gone/

abcdefghijklmnopqrstuvwxyz
ABCDEFGHIJKLMNOPQRSTUVWXYZ
0123456789 [.,:;?!$&-⊗] @"#%'⊕/\ <>= ˆ_`|€

Weights Available: Regular

Designer: Ray Larabie

Website: www.larabiefonts.com

Platform: PC, Mac

Category: Decorative, Sans Serif

Date of Creation: 1999

Additional Information: Other freeware & shareware fonts are available from the same source and commercial fonts are available from the same designer at www.typodermic.com.

Read Me: This font is free to use for personal and/or commercial purposes. No payment is necessary but a sample of your product would be gratefully appreciated so I can see how the font looks in use.

If you'd like to make a voluntary donation to Larabie Fonts for the use of the free fonts in any amount please go to www.larabiefonts.com/donation.html.

Some Larabie fonts have enhanced and expanded families available for sale at: www.typodermic.com.

NB: A complete licence agreement is enclosed with each 'Larabie' font downloaded.

Direct URL: www.myfonts.com/fonts/larabie/zrnic/

Experimental Fonts

N9 (Number Nine) is not exactly a classic foundry, it is a multimedia outfit that uses typography, among other means, to put ideas into action. To us an idea is above all a reflection; a concept that triggers imagination or discussions. The release of a N9 product is not the end of the creative process, but the beginning, and this is what leads us to produce freeware fonts.

While many see freeware fonts as a threat (if you can download fonts for free, why buy commercial fonts?), we see it as a great opportunity to distribute and share our experimentations. Releasing a freeware font is a good way to exchange ideas with users and with other Type Designers. We consider a freeware font to be an idea set free; we release them just like you would formulate a proposal in order to start a discussion.

We do create 'classic' fonts which we sell commercially, but to us typography is above all an extraordinary tool to question things. We create fonts that explore the limits of type, the meaning of the typographic phenomenon and its consequences at a philosophical level.

With Code Elizabeth (N9.018) we have used type to encode an image. The Designer, Guillaume took an image of his wife, converted it into a two tone image and divided it into 256 little squares. A font was then created by replacing each one of the 256 ASCII letters with 1/256th of the picture. Only if you apply the type to the original text do you get the image back and decipher its meaning; any other combination ends up with obscure graphic patterns, in which it is apparent that there should be a meaning (as some parts are decipherable, like half an eye, a section of lip) but which can't be seen as a whole.

Another N9 type, Tu Parles (N9.031), was created by Clarisse Grossier to show how writing can reveal our thoughts. We noticed how people doodle whilst waiting or listening to someone on the telephone. During dull office meetings, people often sketch to put their minds into use. These semi-automatic drawings often express a lot; aggressive whirls when people are nervous, repetitive patterns when people feel the orator is repeating himself, etc. To serve this idea usual communication tools (letters) are replaced by these small, weird, but still meaningful drawings.

What follows are four of our experimental
fonts available for free download:

Anig Gwar (N9.013)

Code Elizabeth (N9.018)

Daedalus (N9.020)

Tu Parles (N9.031)

All of the N9 (Number Nine) commercial
& experimental fonts are available
from: www.n9.fr

Anig Gwar (N9.013)

▢⅄∧⋉⊼⊢⟊⊊⌐⊥⊤⌐⟊⊂∧⋂⋃⋊∏⋁⋋⋌⊼⋎⊞⊊⟊⋊⊤⋌⋉⋋⋇∧⊐⊂
▢⅄∧⋉⊼⊢⟊⊊⌐⊥⊤⌐⟊⊂∧⋂⋃⋊∏⋁⋋⋌⊼⋎⊞⊊⟊⋊⊤⋌⋉⋋⋇∧⊐⊂
⋇∣⊢⊤⊥⊂⊏⋖⊃⋇⊟ ⸢⸢⸍⅄⊠⋔⊹

Weights Available: Light, Regular, Bold

Designer: Guillaume-Ulrich Chifflot

Website: www.n9.fr

Platform: PC, Mac

Category: Experimental

Date of Creation: 1995

Additional Information: Other freeware, shareware and commercial fonts are available from the same source. Please visit the designer's website for more information.

Read Me: The Anig Gwar typeface family and font software are copyright 1995 Guillaume-Ulrich Chifflot for N9.

Anig Gwar is freeware font software, and is exclusively distributed through N9 and is not to be distributed anywhere else or in any way.

NB: A complete licence agreement is enclosed with each 'N9' font downloaded.

Direct URL: www.typeindex.org/hosted/N9/index.php?id=013

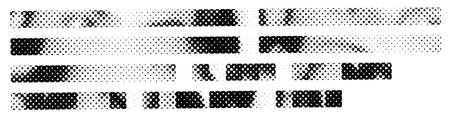

Weights Available: Elizabeth

Designer: Guillaume-Ulrich Chifflot

Website: www.n9.fr

Platform: PC, Mac

Category: Experimental

Date of Creation: 1996

Additional Information: Other freeware, shareware and commercial fonts are available from the same source. Please visit the designer's website for more information.

Read Me: The Code Elizabeth typeface family and font software are copyright 1996 Guillaume-Ulrich Chifflot for N9.

Code Elizabeth is freeware font software, and is exclusively distributed through N9 and is not to be distributed anywhere else or in any way.

NB: A complete licence agreement is enclosed with each 'N9' font downloaded.

Direct URL: www.typeindex.org/hosted/N9/index.php?id=018

Daedalus (N9.020)

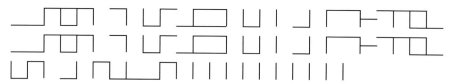

Weights Available: Regular, Bold

Designer: Guillaume-Ulrich Chifflot

Website: www.n9.fr

Platform: PC, Mac

Category: Experimental

Date of Creation: 2003

Additional Information: Other freeware, shareware and commercial fonts are available from the same source. Please visit the designer's website for more information.

Read Me: The Daedalus typeface family and font software are copyright 2003 Guillaume-Ulrich Chifflot for N9.

Daedalus is freeware font software, and is exclusively distributed through N9 and is not to be distributed anywhere else or in any way.

NB: A complete licence agreement is enclosed with each 'N9' font downloaded.

Direct URL: www.typeindex.org/hosted/N9/index.php?id=020

Weights Available: Regular

Designer: Clarisse Grossier

Website: www.n9.fr

Platform: PC, Mac

Category: Experimental

Date of Creation: 2004

Additional Information: Other freeware, shareware and commercial fonts are available from the same source. Please visit the designer's website for more information.

Read Me: The Tu Parles typeface family and font software are copyright 2004 Clarisse Grossier for N9.

Tu Parles is freeware font software, and is exclusively distributed through N9 and is not to be distributed anywhere else or in any way.

NB: A complete licence agreement is enclosed with each 'N9' font downloaded.

Direct URL: www.typeindex.org/hosted/N9/index.php?id=031

Typeindex.org

Typeindex is a community-
based project created with
the intention of building a
definitive index of global
typefaces. Any font lover,
user or author can include
freeware, shareware and
commercial fonts or foundries
to the database. The website
is offered by a non-profit
organisation based in France;
Point Central.

As well as offering typographic
tutorials, typeindex.org is also
a search engine that allows
users to browse through all
the listed fonts using 10
user-oriented criteria.

For more information please
visit: www.typeindex.org

Portrait of a Family

In a time when computers have made Typography a thing anyone can use and abuse, it is a matter of survival for typographic art that users should have a fair knowledge and understanding of Typography.

Even though the elementary approach that follows can't replace academic courses and years of interest in the numerous subtleties of the subject, we've tried to give the basics of our beloved letters, starting with a portrait of a family.

To begin, a 'typeface' (also known as a font) is a complete set of characters drawn in the same way, with the same weight and gathered under a single name. Helvetica demi and Helvetica bold are two distinct typefaces belonging to the same family. Originally, a 'type-face' was the raised surface of a metal character that when pressed to the paper produced a print of the letter.

There are up to 5 different sets of letters within a typeface:

1. The standard characters
   In countries using Roman alphabets the standard set includes (large) capitals, lowercases (regular), numbers, accentuated capitals and lowercases, punctuation signs and various other signs – among which are the monetary symbols and the mathematical symbols. A decent commercial font must have these.

2. Small capitals
   This set features normal capitals, but the lowercases are replaced with small capitals. These small capitals are a redrawn version of the normal capitals at a smaller size. Even if their strokes or stems are slightly thinner than the capitals, they remain homogeneous and are not a whole mathematical reduction. Most graphic software has a 'small caps' function which creates an unpleasant mathematical reduction in much the same way as the 'bold' and 'italic' functions. The use of these functions is not recommended, either for legibility or integrity.

3. Experts

   The expert sets consist of more unusual letters and signs, amongst which are small capitals, complete sets of ligatures, punctuation signs and fractions.

4. Alternates

   Also named Swash capitals this set includes some alternative letters which are scarcely used such as special ligatures, special versions of letters for ending texts and special ornamented capitals.

5. Display sets

   Also known as Tilting capitals, these include versions of the letters specially drawn for use at very large point sizes (such as on posters and display boards) and for being decipherable from a distance. They do not feature lowercases.

To enrich a text layout, and to help Designers to create various levels of legibility most typefaces have several variants:

Italics: An Italic is not to be confused with a slanted typeface (also called an Oblique), as the latter is just a slanted version of the Roman typeface, whereas, unlike a Roman typeface which is vertically constructed, an italic is a version constructed around a slanted axis. The average angle of the Italic is between 7 and 20 degrees, it is far more cursive than the Roman and gives sentences a definite feel of movement. Italic legibility isn't as good as Roman, and therefor it isn't recommended for use in long sentences and is mostly used to emphasise a single word amidst a text or short texts. It also infers a certain intimacy, which is why it is often used to type quotations.

Weight: Varying weights within a family allow the Designer to create contrasts within a layout or to lay emphasis on certain words or sentences. A typeface family articulates around the Roman and each weight variant is carefully redrawn, each one having its own Italic or

Oblique. The main variants are Ultra-light/thin, Light, Demi/Semi-light, Book, Roman/Plain/ Regular/Normal, Medium, Demi/Semi-bold, Bold, Heavy, Black and Ultra-black. Each face generally gets thicker horizontally rather than vertically (to preserve the size of the letter as uniformly as possible from one weight to another) which again is why the 'bold' function of software is inadvisable; it makes the face regularly thicker and so often creates an ugly transformation.

Width: Another variant concerns the width of letters. Originally intended to allow for bigger point sizes within a determined width or height, these variants are Ultra-condensed, Extra-condensed, Condensed, Extended and Wide. Most faces have only a few; mostly an Extended and a Condensed variant. There are also variants named Compressed and Narrow, which feature more pronounced thickness differences between vertical and horizontal strokes.

Rounded: Rounded is a less common variant which deals with rounding the edges of letters.

To conclude, creating a typeface family is long, hard work, often years in the making. With all those variants a Graphic Designer feels like a musician in front of a grand piano with infinite possibilities to create emotions, yet as with music, some good advice is to try to stay simple – and not to use too many variants at the same time!

For the complete tutorial and other tutorials covering creating type, the anatomy of a letterform, a history of type and understanding different font formats visit: www.typeindex.org.

What are ligatures?

For centuries books and posters were printed using movable metal type placed in rows on large wooden trays. Metal type had a problem: it was difficult to properly space certain letters, noticeably 'f' which collided with another 'f', 'i' and 'l'. The solution was to combine these problem characters into a single block of text called a ligature. There were other ligatures too, but the f-ligatures were the most common.

In the age of computers, automatic kerning positions problem letters without the Designer having to give it a second thought. Ligatures have largely disappeared and many fonts don't include them at all in their glyphs tables. If a Designer or Writer wants ligatures other than the standard fi or fl they have to use more sophisticated publishing software or refer to a chart and insert the desired ligature manually — if it's even included with the font.

Thanks to OpenType* format, ligatures are enjoying a renaissance and they're easy for anyone to use. Software that supports OpenType fonts can include dozens, even hundreds of automatic ligature combinations. Called autoligs, these joined letter combinations just appear as they are being typed. There is no need to reference expanded character charts or memorize keyboard shortcuts. The bulk of the work happens with no effort at all. Designers can view the entire autolig library in the glyph table and easily swap out two letter combinations, called digraphs, and even three letter combinations, called trigraphs.

How can autoligs enhance typography?

Autoligs can be used to break up the monotony of repeated letters in fonts where duplication is undesirable. For example; a font that mimics hand-drawn letters is limited by a single obvious flaw; any two or more letters, side by side, will look identical. Autoligs will replace the second repeated letter with an alternate to break up the monotony.

Some fonts have ligatures for larger common letter combinations to further break up the rubber stamp effect. For example: 'the theme'. If you want a different style for each letter combination, autoligs can be applied one of two ways:

Uppercase fonts: use upper and lower case letters and to bring up different autoligs.

Regular fonts: turn off the autoligs feature for one trigraph and leave it on for the second one.

Sinzano**, a font with more than 400 OpenType autoligs, can create distinctive word art with multiple di- and trigraphs to choose from. For example, 'ROSA'S RESTAURANT' has autoligs for 'ro, re, es, est, st, sta, ta, ra, nt' and even 'esta'.

Add variety to graffiti and hand-penned fonts where each letter should look different by virtue of its individual creation. Amienne**, Funboy** and Owned** look authentically penned or painted when using autoligs to create a natural rhythm and flow.

Grungy and textured fonts used to require a lot of work on the part of the Designer, manually swapping alternates (when they were available). Close examination of genuine letter stamps reveals nicks in the letter and specks in the ink which created unique signatures for each individual letter. Autoligs in Meposa**, Stamp** and Zamora** can emulate the worn, often slightly different textural variations and letter shifts that are the hallmark of well-used rubber stamps.

Autoligs can also enhance logos where unusual ligatures create part of the overall visual design. In time, autoligs will become a staple in every Designer's vocabulary and, with OpenType fonts, they're now within every Designer's reach.

Rina and Ray Larabie
larabiefonts.com, typodermic.com
December 2005

*   OpenType format fonts are fully
    supported by Adobe CS Suite for
    both Mac and Windows.

** Licences for these commercial fonts
    are available from www.typodermic.com.

Index

Contributors

066.FONT: www.006.pl

ABC Types: www.roostertypes.com

Abecedarienne: www.abecedarienne.com

Aboutype: www.aboutype.com

Acid Fonts: www.acidfonts.com

ACME: www.acmefonts.net

Adobe: www.store.adobe.com/type

Altemus Creative: www.altemus.com

Altered Ego: www.alteredegofonts.com

Andrij Type: www.andrij.berdyansk.net

Archive Type: www.archivetype.com

Astigmatic: www.astigmatic.com

Astype: www.astype.de

Atomic Media: www.atomicmedia.net

Australian Type Foundry: www.atf.com.au

Balius, Andreu: www.andreubalius.com

Baseline Fonts: www.baselinefonts.com

Bedoodle: www.bedoodle.com

Behaviour: www.behaviourgroup.com

Biltfonts: www.biltfonts.com

Biorust: www.biorust.com

Bitstream: www.bitstream.com

Blambot: www.blambot.com

Blast: www.blast.co.uk

Blue Vinyl Fonts: www.bvfonts.com

Bolt Graphics: www.boltgraphics.com

Büro Destruct: www.bermuda.ch

Burghal Design: www.burghal.com

Buttfaces: www.buttfaces.com

Callaghan, J: www.mickeyavenue.com

Canada Type: www.canadatype.com

Cape-Arcona: www.cape-arcona.com

Castle Type: www.castletype.com

Chank: www.chank.com

Characters: www.characters.nl

Classic Font Company: www.classicfonts.com

Codesign: www.codesign.co.uk

Comicraft: www.comicbookfonts.com

Cool Fonts: www.cool-fonts.com

Costello, Chris: www.costelloart.com

Cubanica: www.cubanica.com

Dalton Maag: www.daltonmaag.com

Die Typonauten: www.typonauten.de

Digitally Branded: www.digitallybranded.com

Dingbatcave: www.dingbatcave.com

DMTR: www.dmtr.org

DSType: www.dstype.com

Dust: www.kuzumi.net

Dutchfonts: www.dutchfonts.com

Elemeno: www.alexandergrecian.com

Elsner+Flake: www.elsner-flake.com

Émigré: www.emigre.com

Emtype Foundry: www.emtype.net

Enrich Design: www.enrichdesign.com

Evertype: www.evertype.com

FSD: www.fsd.it

Fatchair: www.fatchair.com

FDI: www.fonts.info

Feliciano: www.secretonix.pt

Fenotype: www.fenotype.com

Fewell Foundry: www.martinfewell.com

Flat-it: www.flat-it.com

Font Boutique: www.fontboutique.de

Font Boy: www.fontboy.com

Font Bureau: www.fontbureau.com

Font City: www.fontcity.ru

Font Diner: www.fontdiner.com

Fontfabrik: www.fontfabrik.com

FontFont: www.fontfont.com

Font Haus: www.fonthaus.com

Fonthead Design: www.fonthead.com

Fontkingz: www.fontkingz.com

Fontkitchen: www.fontkitchen.com

Fontmill Foundry: www.liddelldesign.com

Font-O-Rama: www.font-o-rama.com

Fontosaurus: www.fontosaurus.com

Fontoville: www.fontoville.com

Fontsite: www.fontsite.com

Fontsmith: www.fontsmith.com

Fountain: www.fountain.nu

Galapagos: www.galapagosdesign.com

Garage Fonts: www.garagefonts.com

Gallo, Gerald: www.graphicsbygallo.com

Gigofonts: www.gigofonts.com

Gosset, Damien: www.daaams.fr.st

Grummedia: www.grummedia.co.uk

Hamburger Fonts: hamburgerfonts.co.uk

Harris – Intertype: www.harris.com

Helldunkel: www.helldunkel.com

Holland Fonts: www.hollandfonts.com

Foundry and Type Designer Directory

House Industries: www.houseind.com

Identikal: www.identikal.com

ITC: www.itcfonts.com

Jazz's Fonts: www.jazz.futurezone.com

Jeremy Tankard Typography: typography.net

Jukebox Type: www.veer.com

Just Another Foundry: justanotherfoundry.com

Just in Type: www.justintype.com.br

JY&A: www.jyanet.com

Konstantynov, Andriy: www.type.pd.com.ua

Lanston Type: www.lanstontype.com

Larabie: www.larabiefonts.com

Lillie, Patricia: www.patricialillie.com

LMD: www.lmstudio.com/fonts/index.htm

Letraset: www.letraset.com

Letter Be: www.fonts.crealit.com

Letterhead Fonts: www.letterheadfonts.com

Letter Perfect: www.letterspace.com

Letterror: www.letterror.com

Linotype: www.linotype.com

Lomax Design: www.jefflomaxdesign.com

Lucas Fonts: www.lucasfonts.com

Mad Irishman Productions: mad-irishman.net

MAD Type: www.madtype.net

Masterfont: www.masterfont.co.il

Maverick Design: www.roostertypes.com

Mergenthaler: www.roostertypes.com

Mini Fonts: www.minifonts.com

Misprinted Type: www.misprintedtype.com

Moonlight: www.moonlighttype.com

Munch Fonts: www.munchfonts.com

Munk, Kenn: www.kennmunk.com

MVB: www.mvbfonts.com

My Fonts: www.myfonts.com

Nerfect: www.nerfect.com

Neufville Digital: www.neufville.com

New Fonts: www.newfonts.com

Newlyn: www.newlyn.com

Nick's Fonts: www.nicksfonts.com

No Bodoni: www.nobodoni.com

Northern Block, The: thenorthernblock.co.uk

Nuevo Deco: www.kumo.swcp.com/graphics/

Omine Type: www.omine.net

Omnibus: www.omnibus.se

Outside the Line: www.outside-the-line.com

P22: www.p22.com

Page Studio Graphics: www.vershen.com

Pampa Type: www.pampatype.com

ParaType: www.paratype.com

Parkinson Type Design: www.typedesign.com

Phil's Fonts: www.philsfonts.com

Pixietype: www.pixietype.com

Pixel Plant: www.thepixelplant.net

Pizzadude: www.pizzadude.dk

Porchez Typofonderie: typofonderie.com

Positype: www.positype.com

Présence Typo: www.presencetypo.com

Pretty: www.houseofpretty.com

PreussTYPE: www.preusstype.com

Process Type: www.processtypefoundry.com

Foundry and Type Designer Directory

Profonts: www.profonts.de

Protimient: www.protimient.com

Providence Type: www.provtype.com

Psy/Ops: www.psyops.com

Puckertype: www.puckertype.com

Quadrat: www.quadrat.com

Quiet Designs Inc: www.quietdesigns.com

Red Rooster Collection: roostertypes.com

Remote Inc: www.remoteinc.net

RAHCreative: www.rahcreative.com

Sander's Conspiracy: www.annette.net

Santos, Ricardo: www.vanarchiv.com

Scangraphic: www.scangraphic-fonts.com

Scriptorium: www.fontcraft.com

Selfbuild Type: www.selfbuildtype.com

Shamrock: www.shamfonts.com

Sherwood Type: www.p22.com

ShinnType: www.shinntype.com

Simonson, Mark: www.ms-studio.com

SparkyType: www.sparkytype.com

StockBucket: www.stockbucket.com

Storm: www.stormtype.com

Studio 37: www.studio37.nl

Subtitude: www.subtitude.com

Sudtipos: www.sudtipos.com

Suitcase Type Foundry: suitcasetype.com

Surfstation: www.surfstation.lu

Swansbury: www.bfhhandwriting.com

SynFonts: www.synfonts.com

T-26: www.t26.com

Tail Spin Studio: www.tailspinstudio.com

Terminal Design: www.terminaldesign.com

TPC: www.testpilotcollective.com

Tetterode: www.tetterode.nl

Tolstrup Pryds Graphics: www.pryds.com

Transkrypt: www.transkrypt.de

The Chase: www.thechase.co.uk

The Microfoundry: themicrofoundry.com

The Type Fetish: www.typefetish.com

Typadelic: www.typadelic.com

TypeArt Foundry: www.typeart.com

Typebox: www.typebox.com

Typeco: www.typeco.com

TypeCulture: www.typeculture.com

TypeSETit: www.typesetit.com

Typetype: www.typetype.net

Type Studio: www.typestudio.com

Typo5: www.typo5.com

Typodermic: www.typodermic.com

Typotheque: www.typotheque.com

Underware: www.underware.nl

UNDT: www.undt.co.uk

Union Fonts: www.unionfonts.com

URW++: www.urwpp.de

Vanderfont: www.vanderfont.com

Verbum: www.verbum.se

Victory Type: www.type.nu

Village: www.vllg.com

Virus: www.virusfonts.com

Visual Mind Rockets: visualmindrockets.com

Foundry and Type Designer Directory

Martin Wait Type: www.martinwaitfonts.com

Wiescher Design: www.wiescher-design.de

Wilton Foundry: robbie.com/wiltonfoundry

Woodruff, Kenneth: kennethwoodruff.com

Woodside Graphics: www.arroyostyle.com

Wundes: www.wundes.com

Y & Y: www.newlyn.com

You Work For Them: youworkforthem.com

Zang-O-Fonts: www.zangofonts.com

Association Typographique: www.atypi.org

Create: www.createmagazine.com

Designerstalk: www.designerstalk.com

Designing with Type: designingwithtype.com

Fonts: www.fonts.com

Fontzone: www.fontzone.com

k10k: www.k10k.net

Luc: jeff.cs.mcgill.ca/~luc/fonts.html

Luminescene: www.luminescene.com

My Fonts: www.myfonts.com

Netdiver: www.netdiver.net

Typeright: www.typeright.org

SOTA: www.typesociety.org

Typographica: www.typographi.com

Acknowledgments

We would like to take this opportunity to thank all the Type Designers, Foundries and Artists who have allowed us to publish their work.

Special credit is due to Mark Simonson for supplying the foreword and to Richard Kegler, also to N9, Typeindex.org and to Ray and Rina Larabie for supplying articles.

Ray Larabie kindly supplied the font Sinzano for use on the cover of this book. Sinzano is a commercial font and a licence can be purchased from typodermic.com.

Special thanks are also due to Nina David at Font-O-Rama for supplying Mein Schatz for use in the body of this publication. This is also a commercial font and a licence can be purchased from font-o-rama.com.

We would also like to mention all the Type Designers who submitted fonts which, for varying reasons, we were unable to include. Your support is very much appreciated.

Thanks are also due to:
Barbara Wilcox – Prince's Trust,
All at SP/ARK,
Carole – Netdiver,
Daniel O'Driscoll,
Tall Kids,
Eduardo Recife – Misprinted Type,
Sébastien – Subtitude,
Racheal – Unwin Brothers,
Igor – Luminescene,

and for creative input to:
Charlotte, Gabrielle, Rachel & Jude.

Steve & Marie Campbell
Début Publications Ltd
February 2006